"Linda Shepherd has hit it out of the park again! What a timely word for those longing to deepen their faith! In this power-packed book, Linda shows you exactly how to pray the promises of Scripture. I need this book and you need this book. I highly recommend that you keep a copy on your nightstand."

Becky Harling, international speaker and author of *How to Listen So People Will Talk* and *Who Do You Say That I Am?*

"If you're looking for a faith-booster, read *Praying God's Promises*. You'll encounter stories of people just like you who needed restored hope, answers to prayer, the presence of God, and courage to make the next right choice. You'll also get Scriptures that will help you claim the promises of God and personalize them for your own situation. In this must-read book, you'll encounter the God of promises, and your life will be enriched, blessed, and encouraged as you agree in prayer with what the Bible says, and then rest in the fact that what he says, he will do."

Carol Kent, speaker and author of *He Holds My Hand: Experiencing God's Presence and Protection*

"Pairing up and powering up prayer with the promises of God and the names of God? Oh my, it just does *not* get more powerful than that. What a great resource we have here from prayer expert Linda Evans Shepherd in *Praying God's Promises*. Hanging on to this one!"

Rhonda Rhea, TV personality, humor columnist, author of 14 books, including *Messy to Meaningful*, *Turtles in the Road*, and *Fix Her Upper*

"Linda's book is more valuable than receiving solid gold, for we receive much more when we pray and trust in God's promises that are so eloquently outlined in these pages."

Karen Whiting, author, international speaker, former TV host, and Bible study teacher

D0110394

"Deeply inspiring and thoroughly practical, *Praying God's Promises* will elevate your prayer life and lift your heart. It opens your eyes to the many promises God offers so you can walk in agreement with your Creator—and that is a powerful place to be."

Julie K. Gillies, author of *From Hot Mess to Blessed: Hope to Propel Your Soul and the Promises That Change Everything* and *Prayers for a Woman's Soul*

"*Praying God's Promises* moves readers from complacent faith to proactive trust in God. In this power-packed book, Linda Evans Shepherd commissions us to stand firm on our Savior's promises and act on our faith. The prayers of agreement at the end of each chapter are a master class on praying through Scripture. I guarantee you won't view God's Word the same after reading this book!"

Sarah Forgrave, author of *Prayers for Hope and Healing: Seeking God's Strength as You Face Health Challenges*

"I always turn to author Linda Evans Shepherd when I'm searching for a book on prayer, and *Praying God's Promises* doesn't disappoint. Once again, her words carry me to the throne of God with authenticity and hope. She also uses these passages and topics to remind me of all the things my heavenly Father has promised. This precious volume will have a permanent resting place on my nightstand, although I'm certain I'll purchase it over and over again to share with those I love."

Edie Melson, award-winning author and director of the Blue Ridge Mountains Christian Writers Conference

"If you've ever wondered about the genuineness of prayer or doubted that prayer works in day-to-day life or questioned whether God listens, Linda Shepherd will help you settle all those nagging questions. She tells intriguing stories of how prayer changed situations and people and helps us see how God might intervene in our lives too. Her use of Scripture to reinforce the power of prayer is exceptional, and each chapter explores how knowing an individual name of God gives us faith and strength. Linda is a great writer and a great prayer warrior. You don't want to miss these insights into *Praying God's Promises*."

Karen Porter, international speaker and author
of *Speak Like Jesus*

"Linda Shepherd expertly gives her reader several benefits. First, she comes alongside the reader with a personal anecdote that helps befriend them. Then she provides a promise that demonstrates God's promise for life's various challenges. Finally, she coaches the reader to understand and personalize the promise—so as to develop a skill that will make Scripture a tool for life."

Janet Holm McHenry, author of 23 books, including
PrayerWalk and *The Complete Guide to the Prayers of Jesus:
What He Prayed and How It Can Change Your Life Today*

"I have been a firm believer in praying God's Word over my life, my marriage, and my family. Now Linda Evans Shepherd helps every reader of *Praying God's Promises* to activate the promises of God so we can all experience the power of God working in our everyday lives. Linda inspires, encourages, and motivates us to be people, like those we read about in the Bible, who actually *live* like we believe in the promises of God by praying them! She makes me excited to pray!"

Pam Farrel, bestselling author of 45 books, including
*Discovering Hope in the Psalms: A Creative Bible Study
Experience* and *A Couple's Journey with God*

Other Books by Linda Evans Shepherd

Winning Your Daily Spiritual Battles:
Living Empowered by the Armor of God

Called to Pray: Astounding Stories of Answered Prayer

The Stress Cure: Praying Your Way to Personal Peace

When You Don't Know What to Pray:
How to Talk to God about Anything

When You Can't Find God:
How to Ignite the Power of His Presence

When You Need a Miracle: How to Ask God for the Impossible

Experiencing God's Presence: Learning to Listen While You Pray

The Potluck Club Cookbook

NOVELS:

The Potluck Club

The Potluck Club: Trouble's Brewing

The Potluck Club: Takes the Cake

The Secret's in the Sauce

A Taste of Fame

Bake until Golden

PRAYING GOD'S PROMISES

THE LIFE-CHANGING POWER
OF PRAYING THE SCRIPTURES

Linda Evans Shepherd

Revell
a division of Baker Publishing Group
Grand Rapids, Michigan

Published by Revell
a division of Baker Publishing Group
PO Box 6287, Grand Rapids, MI 49516-6287
www.revellbooks.com

Printed in the United States of America

Library of Congress Cataloging-in-Publication Data
Names: Shepherd, Linda E., 1957– author.
Title: Praying God's promises : the life-changing power of praying the scriptures / Linda Evans Shepherd.
Description: Grand Rapids : Baker Publishing Group, 2018.
Identifiers: LCCN 2017057409 | ISBN 9780800723897 (pbk.)
Subjects: LCSH: Prayer—Christianity. | God (Christianity)—Promises.
Classification: LCC BV210.3 .S54768 2018 | DDC 248.3/2—dc23
LC record available at https://lccn.loc.gov/2017057409

18 19 20 21 22 23 24   7 6 5 4 3 2 1

In loving memory
of precious Laura

Contents

Introduction

GOD IS A GOD OF PROMISES

> For all of God's promises have been fulfilled in Christ
> with a resounding "Yes!" And through Christ, our
> "Amen" (which means "Yes") ascends to God for his
> glory.
>
> 2 Corinthians 1:20 NLT

Got worries, problems, and uncertainty about the future?

What if God could reach out and send you a message to assure you that he's got everything under control?

He has! God has sent you messages of miracles and hope to help you combat even the worst of life's challenges. The messages I'm referring to are the many promises he has given us in his Word.

Because of God's promises, we know he loves us, he is with us, he will never leave us, and he will fight our battles, heal our diseases, and more.

Do God's promises really make a difference? Yes, especially if you need a breakthrough, hope, confidence, a change of circumstances, healing, comfort, provision, a relationship restored, children blessed, a loved one rescued, or a God who is big enough to trust no matter the size of your problems. God's promises have the power to calm storms, incite miracles, and, best of all, deliver you.

I know God's promises are real, for I am living proof. Let me tell you what happened when I recently put one of God's promises to the test.

My friend Rebecka and I were driving to the airport after a prayer conference when Rebecka clutched her chest. Her face contorted, and she gasped, "I think I'm having a heart attack!"

I sped to a nearby hospital, where the doctors couldn't find a reason for Rebecka's agony and treated her with pain meds much too strong for her system. This caused her to become far worse than when I had first brought her in. Despite her condition, the hospital staff dumped my unconscious friend back into our rental car, saying, "She has a virus, and we need her bed."

Our flight had left without us, so I made my way back to the dark house we'd left earlier that afternoon. Rebecka couldn't walk, and I barely got her inside. As my friend sat on the sofa, she began to talk gibberish to an invisible Sir Gilead. While keeping an eye on Rebecka, I made the beds and unpacked our suitcases. Suddenly, I felt hot, then chilled, and I began to tremble. My muscles ached, and my brain sunk into a fog. *Wait. Am I coming down with the flu too? No! I have to take care of Rebecka. I have to get us back to the airport to catch our new morning flight. If I become ill, we could be stranded here for who knows how long.* I cried out to God, "I really need your help!"

That's when I reached for my Bible and opened it to a psalm that some believe was written by Moses. As I read it, God's promises leapt from the page:

> For he will rescue you from every trap
>> and protect you from deadly disease.
> He will cover you with his feathers.
>> He will shelter you with his wings.
>> His faithful promises are your armor and protection.
> Do not be afraid of the terrors of the night,
>> nor the arrow that flies in the day.
> Do not dread the disease that stalks in darkness,
>> nor the disaster that strikes at midday.
> Though a thousand fall at your side,
>> though ten thousand are dying around you,
>> these evils will not touch you. (Ps. 91:3–7 NLT)

As soon as I read those words, a deep level of trust began to rise in my spirit. God was with me. He would rescue us. Everything was going to be all right.

Within moments of that revelation, my flu symptoms simply vanished. I was able to get Rebecka to her bed and tuck her in for the night.

The next morning was miraculous. I felt fine, and Rebecka was back to her sweet self with no trace of illness. We were able to catch our flight to San Francisco, where we boarded separate flights to our home cities. Rebecka made it without incident to Illinois, and I landed in Denver, still feeling good.

However, when we walked through the doors of our respective houses, the flu bug picked up where it had left off twenty-four hours earlier, and we both ended up with chills, fever, and a hacking cough.

We would have preferred that those symptoms not return, but having a day of wellness in the middle of the flu was nothing short of a miracle. Otherwise, we would have been stranded in a strange city without the help we needed.

I attribute our travel miracle to the promises I read in Psalm 91, for as I read them, the words seemed to jump into my spirit, and I was able to agree with a resounding yes! My yes was the perfect setup for a miracle because my yes to God's promises matched the yes of God's promises.

Are there other promises of God like the ones found in Psalm 91? Yes again! And they apply to all areas of our lives, from breakthroughs to peace, children, marriage, jobs, joy, healing, direction, and much more.

I've mined God's Word for these promises—for you to read, declare, and pray. You can cling to these promises, all of which demonstrate that God is in the mood to say yes to you.

———

God, the Creator, stepped through time and space to scoop his hand into the earth's rich clay to form a man. With his own breath, he breathed life into Adam, and then, from a rib beneath man's heart, God formed Eve. After that, God blessed this couple with his very presence. But when sin ripped Adam and Eve from his holy grasp, he gave them and their descendants his promises—promises of redemption and promises of his enduring love.

God's promises of redemption and enduring love are so glorious that we might think God wouldn't have felt the need to promise anything else. Yet, God lavished us with more promises, promises that can be found throughout his Word. In fact, BibleGateway records over fifty-four hundred divine promises that God made to us. Why did God go to this extreme? He was never obliged to promise us anything, especially that he would send his only begotten Son to die on a rugged cross to pay the price for our sins.

I believe God was motivated to shower us with promises out of his great love for us, his children. The apostle Paul once said, "So now you are not a slave; you are God's child, and God will give you the blessing he promised, because you are his child" (Gal. 4:7 NCV). Because we are God's beloved children, he provided a way so that we would no longer be separated from him on account of his holiness and our sinfulness. He gifted us with promises because he is, by nature, not only a promise maker but also a promise keeper.

And the beauty is that his promises are often activated by our willingness to say yes to him. For example, we say to God:

- Yes, I receive the salvation you provided for me.
- Yes, I believe Jesus died for my sins.
- Yes, I will follow Jesus.
- Yes, I will live my life for you.
- Yes, I will turn from my sins.
- Yes, I want more of the Holy Spirit in my life.
- Yes, I believe your Word.
- Yes, I believe your promises are even for me.

Author Nick Harrison points out that God has a few expectations regarding his promises. He says:

Now as you dig into God's promises remember, God wants you to expect more from him than you're currently experiencing. He wants to be your Provider, Comforter, Counselor, Protector—well your Everything! He's bigger than you can possibly imagine and is able to do "immeasurably more than all we ask or imagine, according to his power that is at work in us" (Eph. 3:20). His promises are his invitation to a happy life.[1]

In other words, God's promises are about drawing you ever nearer to him so that he can lavish his love upon you. Yes, even if you don't deserve it. In fact, God especially wants to draw near to the undeserving and restore their relationship with him. He wants you to rest in him, and he wants to rest his Spirit on you. All you have to do to start this process is to say yes!

1

God's Powerful Promises

The LORD always keeps his promises;
he is gracious in all he does.

Psalm 145:13 NLT

Sometimes I doubt the ministry dreams God has placed on my heart. After all, we're talking about me—a wife and a mom with dirty dishes in the sink, a woman still reeling from a terrible loss. Who am I to think I can make a difference in the lives of people who read my books? I pray about my worry: "Lord, what if these dreams are only my own selfish ambition? Show me whether I'm crazy for believing or just crazy enough to believe you will do the impossible. Show me, Lord. Show me what to believe."

That's when one of God's promises jumps off the page of my Bible and quickens my spirit: "But I have raised you up for this purpose, that I might show you my power and that my name might be proclaimed in all the earth" (Exod. 9:16 NIV).

Yes! That's my dream exactly—to proclaim God's name in all the earth. But wait just a minute. Aren't these the words God told Moses to say to Pharaoh thousands of years before I even existed?

Yes, that's true. But something happens to me as I read Exodus 9:16. It is like the Holy Spirit highlights this verse of Scripture for *me*. And in a moment of time, I go from doubting God's call on my life to believing it is possible, even though I fully understand I am no Pharaoh, much less a Moses, but a Linda with a mission of her own.

Another reason I believe God is speaking to me through this verse is because of the joy I feel in my heart as this verse comes alive to me. I love the idea of lifting up God's name, not in my power but in *his* power.

I have encountered God and his wonderful power many times, and I can't wait to trust him again. And like they say, it's really all about who you know. When you know the promise maker, you can learn to trust his promises. That's why, throughout this book, we will study many of God's names, because when you understand that a loving and powerful God is making you a promise, you can more easily find the faith to believe he wants to move on your behalf. And it is the very moment you believe one of God's promises that God activates that promise over your life.

In each chapter, I will lead you into powerful prayer experiences regarding the promises of God. This step will help you claim and declare each promise so that the power of God can ignite the promise in your life.

Allow God to plant each promise deep into your heart so that you can soon reap the fruit of his promises."

Andrew Murray said, "There is something more necessary than the effort to exercise faith in each separate promise that comes to our attention. That is the cultivation of a trustful attitude toward

God—the habit of always thinking of Him, of His ways and of His works, with bright, confident hopefulness. In such promises alone, the individual promises take root and grow up."[1]

THE PROMISE GARDEN OF GOD'S POWERFUL PROMISES

In our first walk into God's garden of promises, we'll study promises *about* God's promises. Read each promise as well as the following agreement of the promise quietly in your heart or, better yet, out loud. This will help you come into full agreement with God's yes to you.

Your Word says: "For all of God's promises have been fulfilled in Christ with a resounding 'Yes!' And through Christ, our 'Amen' (which means 'Yes') ascends to God for his glory" (2 Cor. 1:20 NLT).

I agree: I love that all of your promises are a yes in Christ. I agree with each promise, fulfilled by Christ himself, with my own yes and amen.

Your Word says: "You know with all your heart and soul that not one of all the good promises the LORD your God gave you has failed. Every promise has been fulfilled; not one has failed" (Josh. 23:14 NIV).

I agree: Lord, my heart and soul trust that every good promise you have given me has not failed but has been fulfilled.

Your Word says: "The LORD always keeps his promises; he is gracious in all he does" (Ps. 145:13 NLT).

I agree: How thankful I am that you, in your graciousness, always keep your promises.

Your Word says: "You are blessed for believing that the Lord would keep his promise to you" (Luke 1:45 GW).

I agree: You, God, are blessing me because I believe you are my promise keeper and will keep all of your promises to me.

Your Word says: "A man cannot please God unless he has faith. Anyone who comes to God must believe that He is. That one must also know that God gives what is promised to the one who keeps on looking for Him" (Heb. 11:6 NLV).

I agree: Lord, I believe you are who you say you are. I please you because I have faith. I have faith in you, and I believe that you will give me all that you've promised me as I continue to seek you.

Dear Lord,

Thank you for these powerful promises. I say yes and agree with them and believe they are for me. Give me even more faith to believe as I cling to your Word. I pray this in the power of the name of Jesus. Yes and amen.

2

Answers to Prayer

I will answer them before they even call to me.
While they are still talking about their needs,
I will go ahead and answer their prayers!

Isaiah 65:24 NLT

Author Catherine Marshall wrote, "Jesus taught that answered prayer requires persistence. There may be a period when a door of blessing remains shut to us. Yet if we persist in knocking, the promise is that God will eventually open the door."[1]

This is exactly what Jesus said in Luke 11:9–10: "And so I tell you, keep on asking, and you will receive what you ask for. Keep on seeking, and you will find. Keep on knocking, and the door will be opened to you. For everyone who asks, receives. Everyone who seeks, finds. And to everyone who knocks, the door will be opened" (NLT).

Marie Underwood understands this promise regarding persistence in prayer. When her daughter graduated from college, she moved five hours away. Not long after her daughter met her boyfriend, they moved in together. Marie said, "Shortly after my daughter married her boyfriend, they gave birth to a son. We saw them maybe only once a year, but there was never any real relationship. As the years went by, our relationship became more stressed and distant. My husband and I knew the kids were living without the Lord, and it broke our hearts. Each day we prayed they would surrender their hearts to the Father."

Marie and her husband, Dale, stood on promises such as Romans 8:38–39, which says:

> And I am convinced that nothing can ever separate us from God's love. Neither death nor life, neither angels nor demons, neither our fears for today nor our worries about tomorrow—not even the powers of hell can separate us from God's love. No power in the sky above or in the earth below—indeed, nothing in all creation will ever be able to separate us from the love of God that is revealed in Christ Jesus our Lord. (NLT)

And God's love broke through. One particular Father's Day, God answered Marie's prayers in a very real way. She explained, "Our daughter called to say that she had fallen on her knees and surrendered her heart to Jesus. God did heart surgery on her that day. She began devouring the Word and applying it to her life."

Marie said, "The road has been hard but worth it. Our daughter has such a testimony of how God can redeem a life from the pit and make it worth living."[2]

Marie saw how a prayer based on a promise, mixed with faith and love, transformed her daughter's life.

Name above All Names

God is a faithful God, and we can see his faithfulness described in his name *Yahweh*, which means "I Am." This name of God was so revered by the Israelites that they regarded it as too sacred to be spoken aloud. This name means that God is faithful. He never changes, nor do his promises fail.

God revealed his name Yahweh to Moses while Moses was complaining about the assignment the Lord had given him to beseech Pharaoh to set his people free. Pharaoh not only rejected Moses's request but also punished God's people by giving them the impossible task of making bricks without straw. So Moses sought the Lord, asking, "Why have you brought all this trouble on your own people, Lord? Why did you send me? Ever since I came to Pharaoh as your spokesman, he has been even more brutal to your people. And you have done nothing to rescue them" (Exod. 5:22–23 NLT).

God answered Moses by introducing his name Yahweh, the Lord. He told Moses that he had heard the cries of his people and that he remembered the covenant he'd made to give them the Promised Land. He told Moses to tell the people:

> I am the Lord. I will free you from your oppression and will rescue you from your slavery in Egypt. I will redeem you with a powerful arm and great acts of judgment. I will claim you as my own people, and I will be your God. Then you will know that I am the Lord your God who has freed you from your oppression in Egypt. I will bring you into the land I swore to give to Abraham, Isaac, and Jacob. I will give it to you as your very own possession. I am the Lord. (Exod. 6:6–8 NLT)

When Moses knocked on heaven's door, God heard him. God hears you too, and he promises to answer you. Let's walk through the promise garden of answers to prayer to discover that:

- God hears
- God answers

THE PROMISE GARDEN
OF ANSWERS TO PRAYER

GOD HEARS

Your Word says: "As for me, I look to the LORD for help. I wait confidently for God to save me, and my God will certainly hear me" (Mic. 7:7 NLT).

I agree: Lord, I look to you for help and wait on you with confidence, because I know you hear me.

***

Your Word says: "I have called upon You, for You will hear me, O God; incline Your ear to me, and hear my speech" (Ps. 17:6 NKJV).

I agree: I am calling on you, Lord, and you hear me. You are leaning in to hear my prayer. Thank you.

***

Your Word says: "The LORD is near to everyone who prays to him, to every faithful person who prays to him. He fills the needs of those who fear him. He hears their cries for help and saves them" (Ps. 145:18–19 GW).

I agree: Lord, you are near to me, especially when I pray. You take care of my needs because I revere and honor you. You hear me when I cry for help and rescue me. Thank you for saving me.

***

Your Word says: "In those days when you pray, I will listen. If you look for me wholeheartedly, you will find me" (Jer. 29:12–13 NLT).

I agree: Lord, it is a relief to know that you have promised to listen when I pray. You promise to be found when I earnestly look for you.

GOD ANSWERS

Your Word says: "I will answer them before they even call to me. While they are still talking about their needs, I will go ahead and answer their prayers!" (Isa. 65:24 NLT).

I agree: You answer me, Lord, because I call on you. How wonderful that you answer me even before I'm finished telling you of my need.

Your Word says: "Call to me, and I will answer you. I will tell you great and mysterious things that you do not know" (Jer. 33:3 GW).

I agree: Lord, it gives me peace to know that when I call on you, you will answer me and help me solve mysteries I need to understand.

Your Word says: "If you abide in Me, and My words abide in you, you will ask what you desire, and it shall be done for you" (John 15:7 NKJV).

I agree: Lord, because you and your words are alive in me, you answer me when I pray.

Your Word says: "Ask, and you will receive. Search, and you will find. Knock, and the door will be opened for you. Everyone who asks will receive. The one who searches will find, and for the one who knocks, the door will be opened" (Matt. 7:7–8 GW).

I agree: What a wonderful promise to cling to as I ask, seek, and knock on heaven's door with my prayers. I know you will answer me, Lord. You will help me receive my request, you will open your door to me, and you will show me your heart for me as well as answers to all of my prayers. I step through your open door with a grateful heart.

Your Word says: "If you do not have wisdom, ask God for it. He is always ready to give it to you and will never say you are wrong for asking" (James 1:5 NLV).

I agree: I never need to be ashamed to come before you with my requests. As I seek you for wisdom, you will show me your way and your truth. You never disapprove of me when I come to you with even small matters. Thank you for your love.

Your Word says: "If you believe, you will receive whatever you ask for in prayer" (Matt. 21:22 NIV).

I agree: I do believe you, Lord Jesus, especially when you said I will receive whatever I ask for in prayer. I know you are Lord. I know you will answer me. I know you will move on my behalf. Thank you!

Your Word says: "Until now you have not asked for anything in my name. Ask and you will receive, and your joy will be complete" (John 16:24 NIV).

I agree: How wonderful that you ask me to make requests of you—in your name. My joy is on the rise, even before I receive my answer from you. It's worth everything to know that you want me to come to you. So I humbly do so now and ask this request that is on my heart in the name of Jesus. (Make your request now.) Thank you for this opportunity.

Your Word says: "They cried out to God during the battle, and he answered their prayer because they trusted in him" (1 Chron. 5:20 NLT).

I agree: Help! The battle is raging around me. But I am safe as I call on you. I am winning this battle with the name of Jesus. I trust this battle to you.

> *Dear Lord,*
>
> *Thank you for these promises that you both hear and answer me. I say yes and agree with them and believe they are for me. Give me even more faith to believe as I cling to your Word. I pray this in the powerful name of Jesus. Yes and amen.*

3

Blessings

The LORD will bless you and watch over you. The LORD
will smile on you and be kind to you. The LORD will
look on you with favor and give you peace.

Numbers 6:24–26 GW

God wants to bless us, to help us rise above our circumstances, to
help us find provision in every lack, to empower us to defeat the
evil one, and to enable us with his power to achieve the purposes
he's set for our lives.

Psalm 40:5 recounts the blessings of God: "You have done many
miraculous things, O LORD my God. You have made many wonderful plans for us. No one compares to you! I will tell others about
your miracles, which are more than I can count" (GW).

Author Rebecka Jordan said:

God does love to bless his people. It is his nature to do so. He
blessed Adam with a companion and gave them both a luxurious
paradise in which to live and fellowship perfectly with their Creator.

28

When sin separated us from Him, God insisted on pouring out His greatest blessing: the gift of His own precious Son as Savior of the world. Relentlessly he pursues us, loves us, and waits for us, so He can bless us even more in a hundred thousand ways.[1]

God wants to bless us, and he wants to bless others through us. This is what my friend Karen realized when she began to bless her young son over forty years ago.

Karen was worried about Brett, who was a bit hyper, so she looked for a promise she could pray over him. She found Psalm 72, which was written by David to bless his son Solomon. Daily she prayed, "Give your love of justice to the king, O God, and righteousness to the king's son. Help him judge your people in the right way; let the poor always be treated fairly" (vv. 1–2 NLT).

How she loved praying that Brett would have good judgment, because he needed it. She also loved praying that God would make him a righteous, good, and godly man who would be fair as he dealt with others.

The psalm continues, "May the mountains yield prosperity for all, and may the hills be fruitful. Help him to defend the poor, to rescue the children of the needy, and to crush their oppressors" (vv. 3–4 NLT).

Whatever mountain Brett climbed, Karen prayed that he would be a peacemaker and that he would defend the afflicted, deliver the needy, and care about those whom no one else would help.

Psalm 72 also includes this verse: "May the people always pray for him and bless him all day long" (v. 15 NLT).

Karen couldn't imagine how this could be possible, that people would pray for her son continually, yet she prayed that they would.

How surprised Karen was when Brett grew up to become a pastor and church planter. His small church built water wells in Haiti, and he and his family work with the underprivileged. Brett defends the afflicted and saves the children, and is there for those no one else will care for, including those who are being trafficked. The people in his church and the church planters he leads love him and constantly keep him in prayer.[2]

How remarkable that David's ancient blessing for his son Solomon became a blessing for Karen's son. God's promises are alive, and Karen activated the promises when she claimed them for Brett. Is it any coincidence that Karen's blessing for Brett became a blessing for people around the globe?

Name above All Names

God is a God of blessings. In fact, one of his names is *El Shaddai*, which means "the Lord God Almighty" or "the Lord of blessings."

According to Genesis 17, God introduced himself to ninety-nine-year-old Abram with this very name. "He said to him, 'I am *El Shaddai*. Continually walk before Me and you will be blameless. My heart's desire is to make My covenant between Me and you, and then I will multiply you exceedingly much'" (vv. 1–2 TLV).

Abram fell on his face before God, and God changed his name from Abram, which means "high father," to Abraham, which means "father of multitudes."

In *The Power of Blessing Your Children*, Mary Ruth Swope wrote, "By becoming members of the family of God, we receive full rights to the blessing of our father, Abraham. And like Abraham, we can pass on God's blessing to our children and grandchildren, just as our forefathers did."[3]

God gave seven blessings to Abraham. We can claim them not only for ourselves but also for our children and grandchildren.

"And I will make you a great nation. I will bring good to you. I will make your name great, so you will be honored. I will bring good to those who are good to you. And I will curse those who curse you. Good will come to all the families of the earth because of you" (Gen. 12:2–3 NLV).

Just as God blessed Abraham, God wants to bless us. He wants to walk with us, his chosen ones. He wants to call us his own. Just as he renamed Abraham, we too have a new identity. We are the redeemed, the beloved, the ones who, like Abraham, walk with God.

Let's take a walk through the promise garden of blessings to discover some of the beautiful blessings that God wants to give to us and through us. Here we will discover promises of:

- God's blessings
- blessing others

THE PROMISE GARDEN OF BLESSINGS

GOD'S BLESSINGS

Your Word says: "The LORD will bless you and watch over you. The LORD will smile on you and be kind to you. The LORD will look on you with favor and give you peace" (Num. 6:24–26 GW).

I agree: You, Lord, are blessing me and watching over me. You smile on me with loving-kindness. You give me favor and peace.

Your Word says: "How abundant are the good things that you have stored up for those who fear you, that you bestow in the sight of all, on those who take refuge in you" (Ps. 31:19 NIV).

31

I agree: Because I revere you and take rest in you, you have stored up good things for me, to be given to me in the sight of everyone. Thank you!

—

Your Word says: "But blessed are those who trust in the LORD and have made the LORD their hope and confidence. They are like trees planted along a riverbank, with roots that reach deep into the water. Such trees are not bothered by the heat or worried by long months of drought. Their leaves stay green, and they never stop producing fruit" (Jer. 17:7–8 NLT).

I agree: I am blessed because I trust in you, Lord, for you are my hope and confidence. I am blessed because I am like a tree on the riverbank. My thirsty roots are continually refreshed. I stay cool in the summer heat and I am able to stay productive, doing all you have called me to do.

—

Your Word says: "Whoever gives attention to the LORD's word prospers, and blessed is the person who trusts the LORD" (Prov. 16:20 GW).

I agree: Lord, I pay attention to your Word, and you prosper me. Not only that, but I am blessed because I trust you.

—

Your Word says: "Blessed is the person who does not follow the advice of wicked people, take the path of sinners, or join the company of mockers" (Ps. 1:1 GW).

I agree: You are blessing me, Lord, because I do not follow advice from wicked people, follow after sinners, or join those who mock others. Help me to continue to follow you and to stay far from deceit.

BLESSING OTHERS

Your Word says: "But love your enemies, do good to them, and lend to them without expecting to get anything back. Then your reward will be great, and you will be children of the Most High, because he is kind to the ungrateful and wicked. Be merciful, just as your Father is merciful" (Luke 6:35–36 NIV).

I agree: Lord, I will love my enemies and do good to them, even lending to them without expecting to get anything back. My reward will be great, and I will be your child, for you, Lord, are kind to the ungrateful and wicked. Help me to follow your example so that I will be merciful as you are merciful to me.

Your Word says: "Don't pay people back with evil for the evil they do to you, or ridicule those who ridicule you. Instead, bless them, because you were called to inherit a blessing" (1 Pet. 3:9 GW).

I agree: Lord, keep my eyes focused on you and your ways. Then I will not pay back the evil done to me or make sport of those who have made sport of me. I will bless them because you called me to inherit a blessing.

Your Word says: "A generous person will prosper; whoever refreshes others will be refreshed" (Prov. 11:25 NIV).

I agree: Lord, how wonderful that you promise that if I am generous, I will prosper, and if I refresh others, I will be refreshed.

—

Your Word says: "God can give you all you need. He will give you more than enough. You will have everything you need for yourselves. And you will have enough left over to give when there is a need" (2 Cor. 9:8 NLV).

I agree: Lord, you give me all I need, more than enough. I will have enough left over to bless others by giving them what they need.

—

Your Word says: "Don't forget to do good things for others and to share what you have with them. These are the kinds of sacrifices that please God" (Heb. 13:16 GW).

I agree: I want to please you, Lord, so I will remember to practice kindness to others, sharing what I have.

—

Dear Lord,

Thank you for these promises of your blessings for me and for others. I say yes and agree with them and believe they are for me. Give me even more faith to believe as I cling to your Word. I pray this in the power of the name of Jesus. Yes and amen.

4

Breakthroughs

We will shout for joy in your victory and lift up our
banners in the Name of our God! May Adonai fulfill
all your petitions.

Psalm 20:6 TLV

You win! You win because you are under God's victorious banner.

Do you know why this is true? It is because the God you serve
is a God of breakthroughs and victory.

In his book *The Applause of Heaven*, Max Lucado said:

Imagine you are an ice skater in a competition. You are in first
place with one more round to go. If you perform well the trophy
is yours. You are nervous, anxious, and frightened.

Then only minutes before your performance, your trainer rushes
to you with the thrilling news: "You've already won! The judges
tabulated the scores, and the person in second place can't catch
you. You are too far ahead."

Upon hearing that news, how will you feel? Exhilarated!

And how will you skate? . . . How about courageously and confidently. You bet you will. You will do your best because the prize is yours. You will skate like a champion because that is what you are. You will hear the applause of victory.[1]

This is also your story. You have already won the battle. Therefore, you can confidently claim the victory.

This may be true, but we don't always pray as if we believe it.

My prayer partner Carole and I have prayed together for the past ten years, seeking God about one urgent matter after another. Carole admits that when we first began to pray together, she was worried that God wouldn't answer her prayers because she thought he wanted her to suffer because of her past mistakes. She was even afraid she wasn't good enough and God would ignore her pleas for help.

But as we prayed, God miraculously answered our prayers with one breakthrough after another. As God continued to give us victory, he began to show Carole that she was truly loved and forgiven and that he wanted to answer her prayers. Our prayers also went through a transformation. When we first started to pray together, our prayers were based more on worry than on faith. Now we're finally able to pray, "Lord, the battle is yours."

Today the answers we seek come faster than ever. We've been privileged to see God move some pretty big mountains. But the key to our breakthroughs was not our personal holiness, our great faith, or even our endearing personalities. We simply sought God, and he lovingly responded.[2]

As Max Lucado wrote, "God's help is near and always available, but it is only given to those who seek it."[3]

Name above All Names

Adonai Nissi means "the Lord is my banner." When Moses was leading his people to the Promised Land, the Amalekite army came against them in the desert (Exod. 17:8–16). Moses came up with an amazing battle plan. He appointed Joshua to lead the Israelite army while he climbed a hill. There on the hilltop, Moses lifted his hands to heaven. As long as his hands were raised, Israel prevailed in the battle. But when Moses's strength failed, his hands dropped and the Amalekites prevailed.

Moses finally became so exhausted that he sat down on a rock, and he allowed his companions to hold up his hands to the Lord. His hands held steady until the Israelites won the battle just as the sun slid beneath the horizon.

Afterward, Moses built an altar to God and called it *Adonai Nissi*, the Lord is my banner.

The Lord is also your banner. Open your heart to him and watch him provide the breakthroughs you need to win the battles you are facing.

Allow the following promises in the promise garden of breakthroughs to strengthen your faith.

THE PROMISE GARDEN
OF BREAKTHROUGHS

Your Word says: "The Lord your God is with you, a Powerful One Who wins the battle. He will have much joy over you. With His love He will give you new life. He will have joy over you with loud singing" (Zeph. 3:17 NLV).

I agree: I am so grateful that you are my Lord God, the powerful One who wins my battles. You are happy to be with me. You pour your love into me and give me new life. You sing with joy over me because I am yours.

Your Word says: "Dear children, you belong to God. So you have won the victory over these people, because the one who is in you is greater than the one who is in the world" (1 John 4:4 GW).

I agree: I do belong to you. You give me victory over my enemies simply because you are in me and you are greater than the one who is in the world.

Your Word says: "With God we will gain the victory, and he will trample down our enemies" (Ps. 60:12 NIV).

I agree: I do not go into the battle alone. I go with you. You give me victory, and you trample down my enemies.

Your Word says: "I put no trust in my bow, my sword does not bring me victory; but you give us victory over our enemies, you put our adversaries to shame" (Ps. 44:6–7 NIV).

I agree: I don't trust human strategies for victory. I trust in you, the God of victory who helps me to defeat my enemies and put my adversaries to shame.

Your Word says: "The God of peace will soon crush Satan under your feet. The grace of our Lord Jesus be with you" (Rom. 16:20 NIV).

I agree: How glad I am that your grace is with me and that you, the God of peace, will crush Satan under my feet.

Your Word says: "The one who loves us gives us an overwhelming victory in all these difficulties" (Rom. 8:37 GW).

I agree: You love me and give me overwhelming victory in all of my difficulties.

Your Word says: "Don't be afraid! Don't be paralyzed by this mighty army! For the battle is not yours, but God's" (2 Chron. 20:15 TLB).

I agree: I am not afraid. I am not paralyzed by fear because of the size of the enemy before me. For the battle belongs to you, Lord, not to me! You have won!

Your Word says: "Finally, be strong in the Lord and in his mighty power. Put on the full armor of God, so that you can take your stand against the devil's schemes. For our struggle is not against flesh and blood, but against the rulers, against the authorities, against the powers of this dark world and against the spiritual forces of evil in the heavenly realms" (Eph. 6:10–12 NIV).

I agree: I am strong in you and in your mighty power. I am putting on Jesus as my armor. In this manner, I will stand against the schemes of the devil, for I am not fighting against people but against evil rulers and authorities, against dark powers and spiritual forces of evil that lurk above the earth and below heaven.

Dear Lord,

Thank you for these promises regarding breakthroughs. I say yes and agree with them and believe they are for me. Give me even more faith to believe as I cling to your Word. I pray this in the power of the name of Jesus. Yes and amen.

5

Children

I will save your children.

Isaiah 49:25 GW

Author Mary Ruth Swope wrote, "We can expect God to do great and marvelous deeds when we call forth the promise of His Word for our loved ones. As you bless your children in the name of the Lord, you will see God fill their lives with good things and bring full Salvation even unto your children's children."[1]

This is true, even when our kids go astray. I was recently chatting with a young man at a prayer conference who shared his story with me. "I was in a gang, dealing drugs on the streets of Chicago," he said. "I was sent to prison three times."

"How did you get from prison to this prayer meeting?" I asked.

"One day I was sitting in my cell, and I said to myself, *What am I doing here? I grew up in the church. I know God, and I'm going back to him.* And so I did."

"I bet you had a praying mother back home."

"My mom prayed constantly for me."

"I bet she claimed a Scripture passage over you, didn't she?"

"Yes! She claimed Proverbs 22:6: 'Train up a child in the way he should go, and when he is old he will not depart from it'" (NKJV).

I grinned. "That's what I guessed! And look at you!"

"I credit my mom and how she held on to that promise from the Lord."

God loves both this mom and her son. Understanding that God loves our children is a great comfort when we pray for them. We can see God's love for his children in his wonderful names.

Name above All Names

One of the names Jesus called God was the Aramaic word *Abba*, meaning "Father God." We also see this name used in Romans 8:15, where the apostle Paul wrote, "For you did not receive the spirit of slavery to fall again into fear; rather, you received the Spirit of adoption, by whom we cry, "*Abba*! Father!" (TLV).

God loves us as a dear father loves his children. He loves us so much that he adopted us into his kingdom.

God loves not only us but also our children. So does Jesus. He spent time blessing a group of children despite his disciples' protests that he didn't have time to do so. Jesus told his men, "'Don't push these children away. Don't ever get between them and me. These children are at the very center of life in the kingdom. Mark this: Unless you accept God's kingdom in the simplicity of a child, you'll never get in.' Then, gathering the children up in his arms, he laid his hands of blessing on them" (Mark 10:14–16 Message).

Jesus loves our children, and he desires for us to raise our children to love him and to know him. He loves the prayers we pray on their behalf. Let's walk through the promise garden for children and claim a few of the many wonderful promises in the Word concerning children for our own kids.

THE PROMISE GARDEN FOR CHILDREN

Your Word says: "Hallelujah! Blessed is the person who fears the LORD and is happy to obey his commands. His descendants will grow strong on the earth. The family of a decent person will be blessed" (Ps. 112:1–2 GW).

I agree: Thank you! I am blessed because I fear you. I am happy to obey your commands. My descendants will grow strong on the earth. My family will be blessed.

⁓

Your Word says: "There is strong trust in the fear of the Lord, and His children will have a safe place" (Prov. 14:26 NLV).

I agree: Because I revere you, Lord, I know I can trust you and that my children will be safe.

⁓

Your Word says: "All your children will be taught by the LORD, and great will be their peace" (Isa. 54:13 NIV).

I agree: Praise be to you, Lord. You will teach my children and will also give them great peace.

⁓

Your Word says: "They will not work in vain, and their children will not be doomed to misfortune. For they are people blessed by the LORD, and their children, too, will be blessed" (Isa. 65:23 NLT).

I agree: My work will not be for nothing, and my children will not be doomed to trouble. I'm delighted that my kids and their kids will be blessed by you, Lord.

Your Word says: "The children of your servants will live in your presence; their descendants will be established before you" (Ps. 102:28 NIV).

I agree: My children will live in your presence, and their descendants will follow you.

Your Word says: "'This is my promise to them,' says the LORD. 'My Spirit, who is on you, and my words that I put in your mouth will not leave you. They will be with your children and your grandchildren permanently,' says the LORD" (Isa. 59:21 GW).

I agree: You promise that your Spirit will be on me, that your Word will come from my mouth. You promise never to leave me and to be forever with my children and grandchildren. Thank you.

Your Word says: "I will bless the thirsty land by sending streams of water; I will bless your descendants by giving them my Spirit. They will spring up like grass or like willow trees near flowing streams. They will worship me and become my people. They will write my name on the back of their hands" (Isa. 44:3–5 CEV).

I agree: You, Lord, promise to bless the thirsty land with streams of living water. You will also bless my descendants with your Holy Spirit. Because my children belong to you, they will flourish as they worship you. Your name will be imprinted upon their hands and their hearts.

Your Word says: "Train up a child in the way he should go, and when he is old he will not depart from it" (Prov. 22:6 NKJV).

I agree: I will train my children to follow you and do right, and when they are grown, they will stay on the right track and follow you and your commands.

Your Word says: "So don't be afraid. I am here. I will reunite you with your children, bringing them back from wherever in the world they are—East, West, North, or South. No place will be able to hold you when I demand your release, when I order them, 'Bring My children—My sons and daughters—from far away. Bring the ones who are called by My name; the ones I made, shaped, and created for My profound glory'" (Isa. 43:5–7 Voice).

I agree: I am not afraid, because you are here. You will reunite me with my children and bring back my sons and daughters from faraway places. You will bring back my kids because they are called by your name. You will help them live into your profound glory.

Your Word says: "This is what the LORD says: Prisoners will be freed from mighty men. Loot will be taken away from tyrants. I will fight your enemies, and I will save your children" (Isa. 49:25 GW).

I agree: You promise that prisoners will escape their captors, treasure will be taken from tyrants, and you will fight my enemies and save my children. Amazing!

Your Word says: "Believe in the Lord Jesus, and you and your family will be saved" (Acts 16:31 GW).

I agree: I praise you, God! Because I believe in the Lord Jesus, my family and I are saved.

Dear Lord,

Thank you for these promises for my children. I say yes and agree with them and believe they are for me. Give me even more faith to believe as I cling to your Word. I pray this in the power of the name of Jesus. Yes and amen.

6

Comfort

I will turn their mourning into joy. I will comfort them.
I will give them joy in place of their sorrow.

Jeremiah 31:13 GW

As a child, when I was sick, my mother would comfort me. She would wrap me in her arms and gently kiss the top of my head. I well remember the feeling of her love and care. How I love that our God is a comforting God. When we stumble, he's there to help us stand. When we fail, he's there to encourage us. When we are going through suffering, he's there to wrap his arms of love around us and take our suffering upon himself.

There are times we all need comfort, and how wonderful it is that we have a Comforter. He is there when we need him most. Thomas Watson said in the book *One Minute Promises of Comfort*, "When God lays men on their backs, then they look up to heaven."[1] Oh, what a glorious view!

Could it be that the joy of a difficulty is that it puts us in a position to not only see God but also watch him move on our behalf?

Steve Miller said, "And His help is never too little or too late. We may not understand His ways or His timing. But we *can* trust Him who made heaven and earth. He who made all can *do* all. Look to Him alone, and help will come."[2]

My friend Bobbie discovered God's arms of comfort. She had been depressed since she'd lost her kids. But when her mother died, she was awakened to even deeper grief, triggering the first of her many suicide attempts. She stumbled through the next fifteen years of her life, battling depression and wishing she were dead.

Finally, one November, Bobbie planned what was to be her last suicide attempt. That Friday night Bobbie swallowed a large dose of an extremely toxic substance. As she began to sicken, one of her praying friends called to tell her how precious she was. Her friend even managed to talk her into going to the ER. From there, Bobbie was admitted into a psychiatric hospital.

A week later, she was released with nowhere to go—no home, not even a job. Miraculously, a friend invited her to move in. Then a few months later, Bobbie got called to go back to her old job. Soon she was able to get a place of her own. Bobbie felt God's comfort as the pieces of her life began to fall into place.

Today, Bobbie continues to live under the grace of God's comfort. Her mother is still gone, she and her kids are still apart, but she feels the arms of God around her. She says, "I have no anxiety or guilt. The way I feel now reminds me of the joy I felt the day I got saved and invited Jesus into my life. This is a feeling that words could never describe. My thoughts are positive. I no longer feel dependent on others for security or approval." She admits, "I still have down days. I miss my mom and my kids, but I don't fall into a deep depression like I used to. Loss is part of life, not an end to life. I can move on, knowing I have friends as well as a God who lifts me up and shines the light into the darkness."

Bobbie explains, "Jesus took the guilt I felt for trying to end my life for fifteen years, and now my life has completely turned around. In fact, life now feels 'normal.' I no longer need antidepressants, anxiety medication, or meds to treat mental illness. I have been promoted to team leader in a job I love. I'm happier than I've been my whole life. I have wonderful friends, and I have a more active social life than ever before. God has definitely answered my prayers. I owe everything to him."[3]

Name above All Names

One of God's names is Comforter.

Imagine the scene. Jesus is sitting around the campfire, knowing he is on a collision course with his destiny, the cross. He knows his death on the cross is necessary if he is going to defeat sin and death so that humankind can be restored to God. But he also knows that his disciples won't understand. So ever so gently, Jesus begins to tell them he is going away. He explains, "When the Father sends the Comforter—and by the Comforter I mean the Holy Spirit—he will teach you much and will remind you of everything I myself have told you."

The Comforter, or the Holy Spirit, had been on earth before. This Spirit of God had rested on the prophets of old, giving them the ability to prophesy, and he had rested on Jesus, in the form of a dove, when John the Baptist baptized Jesus in the Jordan River. Now, Jesus is telling his disciples that this Holy Spirit, the *Ruach HaKodesh*, will come to them and comfort them, teach them, and remind them of his words.

John the apostle later explained to the early Christians, "But you belong to God, my dear children. You have already won a victory over those people, because the Spirit who lives in you is greater than the spirit who lives in the world" (1 John 4:4 NLT).

The Holy Spirit is a wonderful Comforter. Let's tour the promise garden of comfort to see what promises God has made to us regarding his comfort in times of trouble, grief, and suffering.

THE PROMISE GARDEN OF COMFORT

Your Word says: "Blessed are those who mourn. They will be comforted" (Matt. 5:4 GW).

I agree: You bless me when I mourn and give me your comfort.

Your Word says: "The Lord is near to those who have a broken heart. And He saves those who are broken in spirit" (Ps. 34:18 NLV).

I agree: My dear Lord, you are near to me when my heart is broken. You save me when I have a broken spirit.

Your Word says: "Give your burdens to the LORD, and he will take care of you. He will not permit the godly to slip and fall" (Ps. 55:22 NLT).

I agree: When I give you my burdens, you take care of me. You will not permit me to slip and fall.

Your Word says: "Weeping may last through the night, but joy comes with the morning" (Ps. 30:5 NLT).

I agree: Even when I weep through the night, you fill me with your joy in the morning.

Your Word says: "I will turn their mourning into joy. I will comfort them. I will give them joy in place of their sorrow" (Jer. 31:13 GW).

I agree: You promise to comfort me and turn my mourning into joy. My life is transformed because you give me joy in place of my sorrow.

Your Word says: "God our Father loved us and by his kindness gave us everlasting encouragement and good hope. Together with our Lord Jesus Christ, may he encourage and strengthen you to do and say everything that is good" (2 Thess. 2:16–17 GW).

I agree: You are God my Father, and through your kindness, you give me everlasting encouragement and hope. May Jesus himself encourage and strengthen me to do and say everything that is good.

Your Word says: "The LORD helps the fallen and lifts those bent beneath their loads" (Ps. 145:14 NLT).

I agree: You help me when I fall and lift me when I am struggling under a heavy load.

Your Word says: "Praise be to the God and Father of our Lord Jesus Christ, the Father of compassion and the God of all comfort, who comforts us in all our troubles, so that we can comfort those in any trouble with the comfort we ourselves receive from God" (2 Cor. 1:3–4 NIV).

I agree: I praise you, God and Father of my Lord Jesus Christ. You are the Father of compassion. You gift me with comfort in my troubles and enable me to gift this same comfort to others.

—

Your Word says: "Even when I walk through the darkest valley, I will not be afraid, for you are close beside me. Your rod and your staff protect and comfort me" (Ps. 23:4 NLT).

I agree: When I find myself in the darkest valley, I am not afraid, for I know you are close beside me, ready and equipped to protect and comfort me.

—

Your Word says: "Then, when our dying bodies have been transformed into bodies that will never die, this Scripture will be fulfilled: 'Death is swallowed up in victory'" (1 Cor. 15:54 NLT).

I agree: When my time comes to enter into your presence, you will transform my body of death into a body that will never die. Because of you, death is swallowed up in victory.

—

Your Word says: "For He has not turned away from the suffering of the one in pain or trouble. He has not hidden His face from him. But He has heard his cry for help" (Ps. 22:24 NLV).

I agree: You have heard my cry for help. You have not turned from my suffering, pain, or trouble and have allowed me to see your face.

⸺

Your Word says: "Those who cry while they plant will joyfully sing while they harvest. The person who goes out weeping, carrying his bag of seed, will come home singing, carrying his bundles of grain" (Ps. 126:5–6 GW).

I agree: The tears I've planted will bloom into a harvest. I went out weeping, carrying the seed you gave me. I will soon enjoy the fruits of all my labor.

⸺

Your Word says: "He heals those who have a broken heart. He heals their sorrows" (Ps. 147:3 NLV).

I agree: You heal my broken heart as well as my sorrows.

⸺

Dear Lord,

Thank you for these promises regarding comfort. I say yes and agree with them and believe they are for me. Give me even more faith to believe as I cling to your Word. I pray this in the power of the name of Jesus. Yes and amen.

7

Deliverance

Behold, I give unto you power to tread on serpents and
scorpions, and over all the power of the enemy: and
nothing shall by any means hurt you.

Luke 10:19 KJV

What if our promise-keeping God could defeat any demon from
hell, cure any addict, free any lost soul, and deliver us from our
enemies? Carol Graham knows that God is a God who can do all
of this and more.

One warm evening about midnight, she and her husband stepped
onto their back deck. Carol said, "Almost immediately, our cat
took off running into the bushes. In less than a second, we saw a
huge mountain lion take two leaps toward us.

"The cougar was in midair when the promise of protection
rose up in my husband's spirit. In his mind, he was saying Luke
10:19: 'Behold, I give unto you power to tread on serpents and

scorpions, and over all the power of the enemy: and nothing shall by any means hurt you' (KJV).

"My husband only had time to point his finger at the big cat and say, 'In the name . . .' The mountain lion spun 180 degrees in midair and ran in the opposite direction.

"Days later, a conservation officer told us that they captured the big cat who had been on a killing spree. He was the largest one they had ever seen, over 250 pounds."

What does Carol have to say about the incident? She says, "Thank God for the authority he gives us."[1]

God gives us authority in him and in his Word. When we wield the power of this authority, he will deliver us from any attack from the enemy.

And don't get comfortable in the pits of life. Author Beth Moore said, "Quit trying to make the best of it. It's time to get out. When Christ said, 'Come follow me,' inherent in His invitation to come was the equivalent invitation to leave."[2]

It's time to step out of your pits! God truly is a God who wants to deliver you.

Name above All Names

Another name for God is *Migdol Yeshu'ot*, which is Hebrew for "tower of deliverance." What a beautiful picture. God is a tower that will protect us, even deliver us from our enemies.

When we look at 2 Samuel 22:51, the picture gets even brighter. This passage says, "He is a tower of deliverance to His king, and shows lovingkindness to His anointed, to David and his descendants forever" (NASB). God delivers his anointed with loving-kindness—time and time again.

God rescued David from his enemies many times. Not once do we read that God slapped his forehead and exclaimed, "Oy vey, David! Now what?"

God doesn't get impatient with us either. God rescued David out of love, and he will do the same for us.

You may be thinking, *Well, that was David. Of course God loved and rescued him. I bet God knows that I am no David.*

Do you believe that God applies a different, harsher set of rules to you and your troubles than he did to David?

Let's look at the facts:

- God loves you and sent his Son Jesus to die for you.
- Jesus died for you because he loves you.
- Jesus died for you while you were still a sinner.
- He knows you are not perfect, and yet he still loves you.

Do not assume that God thinks the worst about you, that he's sick of you, or that he laughs at you behind your back. God isn't like that. He is a God who loves you. He is a God who delivers you.

Perhaps it's time to lean into God's love as well as his promises of deliverance.

THE PROMISE GARDEN OF DELIVERANCE

Your Word says: "Call upon Me in the day of trouble; I will deliver you, and you shall glorify Me" (Ps. 50:15 NKJV).

I agree: I am calling on you now, Lord. You will deliver me, and I will praise your name!

Your Word says: "When the righteous cry for help, the L ORD hears and delivers them out of all their troubles" (Ps. 34:17 ESV).

I agree: I am blessed, for when I cry for help, you hear and deliver me out of all my troubles.

Your Word says: "Everyone who calls on the name of the L ORD will be saved" (Rom. 10:13 NLT).

I agree: Precious Lord, I call on your name, and I am saved.

Your Word says: "But the Lord is faithful, and he will strengthen you and protect you from the evil one" (2 Thess. 3:3 NIV).

I agree: You are so faithful, Lord. You are strengthening me as you protect me from the evil one.

Your Word says: "Yes, and the Lord will deliver me from every evil attack and will bring me safely into his heavenly Kingdom. All glory to God forever and ever! Amen" (2 Tim. 4:18 NLT).

I agree: Thank you, Lord. You deliver me from every evil attack and bring me safely into your heavenly kingdom. All glory to you, God, forever and always!

Your Word says: "No evil will conquer you; no plague will come near your home. For he will order his angels to protect you wherever you go. They will hold you up with their hands so you won't even hurt your foot on a stone" (Ps. 91:10–12 NLT).

I agree: No evil will conquer me, no plague will come near my home, for you, Lord, order your angels to protect me wherever I go. The angels hold me up with their hands so that I won't even stub my toe.

⁓

Your Word says: "You will not have to fight this battle. Take up your positions; stand firm and see the deliverance the LORD will give you, Judah and Jerusalem. Do not be afraid; do not be discouraged. Go out to face them tomorrow, and the LORD will be with you" (2 Chron. 20:17 NIV).

I agree: I don't have to fight this battle. I'm standing in place, watching you deliver me, Lord. I am not afraid or discouraged.

⁓

Your Word says: "You are my hiding place; you will protect me from trouble and surround me with songs of deliverance" (Ps. 32:7 NIV).

I agree: You hide me from my enemies, Lord. You protect me from trouble as you sing songs that deliver me.

⁓

Your Word says: "The temptations in your life are no different from what others experience. And God is faithful. He will not allow the temptation to be more than you can stand. When you are tempted, he will show you a way out so that you can endure" (1 Cor. 10:13 NLT).

I agree: I experience temptations, the same as everyone else. But you, Lord, are faithful. You will not allow my temptations to be more than I can stand. When I am tempted, you will show me a way out so that I can continue to stand strong.

Your Word says: "Behold, I give unto you power to tread on serpents and scorpions, and over all the power of the enemy: and nothing shall by any means hurt you" (Luke 10:19 KJV).

I agree: Lord, you have given me power to tread on all slithering associates of the enemy. In fact, you give me power over the enemy, and therefore, nothing will hurt me in any way.

Dear Lord,

Thank you for these promises of deliverance. I say yes and agree with them and believe they are for me. Give me even more faith to believe as I cling to your Word. I pray this in the power of the name of Jesus. Yes and amen.

8

Direction

Call to me, and I will answer you. I will tell you great
and mysterious things that you do not know.

Jeremiah 33:3 GW

Amy and her husband needed God's direction. They'd been trying
to adopt a child for years with no luck. Amy prayed continually
for God's will as she clung to promises such as Proverbs 3:5–6:
"Trust in the LORD with all your heart; do not depend on your
own understanding. Seek his will in all you do, and he will show
you which path to take" (NLT).

One day Amy and her husband happened to sit beside a couple
at church with a beautiful little girl. The couple told her they'd
adopted their daughter through the state Human Services Program,
an adoption program Amy hadn't known about. As she listened to
this couple's story, she felt God was showing her that there were
plenty of children who needed someone to love them. Though
Amy and her husband never crossed paths with this couple again,

they soon contacted the Human Services Program and eventually adopted a three-year-old boy and his four-year-old sister who'd been placed in the system.

Today the children are preteens and doing well. Amy is so grateful to God for his direction, which brought these children into her life.[1]

God had a plan for Amy and her husband all along. He can even take a direction we believe is a wrong turn and use it to lead us to joy and his purpose.

Catherine Marshall said in her book *Moments that Matter*, "When we ask God to guide us, we have to accept by faith that He is doing so. This means that when He closes a door in our faces, we do well not to try to crash that door. Sensitivity is needed here. The promise is the Shepherd will go ahead of the sheep; His method is to clear the way for us."[2]

Let's allow God to lead us as our Shepherd.

Name above All Names

Another name for God is *Jehovah Rohi*, which means "the Lord is my shepherd." We can see this description of God in the first verse of Psalm 23, written by King David, a former shepherd himself: "The LORD is my shepherd. I am never in need" (GW).

The job of a shepherd hasn't changed much since David's day. The shepherd protects his flock from predators. He leads his flock to grassy pastures and cool waters. He helps his sheep stay calm and leads them to rest in the cool shade.

God directs us in the same way. Psalm 23 continues, "He makes me lie down in green pastures. He leads me beside peaceful waters. He renews my soul. He guides me along the paths of righteousness for the sake of his name" (Ps. 23:2–3 GW).

Let's walk through the promise garden of direction to discover the promises God our Shepherd has given us regarding his direction in our lives.

The Promise Garden of Direction

Your Word says: "He tends his flock like a shepherd: He gathers the lambs in his arms and carries them close to his heart; he gently leads those that have young" (Isa. 40:11 NIV).

I agree: You tend to me like a good shepherd. You gather me in your arms and carry me close to your heart. You gently lead my children and me.

Your Word says: "Call to me, and I will answer you. I will tell you great and mysterious things that you do not know" (Jer. 33:3 GW).

I agree: When I call to you, you always answer me. You tell me great and mysterious things I need to know.

Your Word says: "Trust in the LORD with all your heart; do not depend on your own understanding. Seek his will in all you do, and he will show you which path to take" (Prov. 3:5–6 NLT).

I agree: Why should I trust in my own understanding when I can trust in you? I seek your will in everything, and in return, you show me which path to take.

Your Word says: "The LORD directs the steps of the godly. He delights in every detail of their lives. Though they stumble, they will never fall, for the LORD holds them by the hand" (Ps. 37:23–24 NLT).

I agree: Where would I be if you did not direct my steps? You delight in every detail of my life. I don't fall when I stumble because you are holding my hand.

⁓

Your Word says: "I know the plans that I have for you, declares the LORD. They are plans for peace and not disaster, plans to give you a future filled with hope" (Jer. 29:11 GW).

I agree: Lord, you have already arranged the plans for my life. They are good plans, not for disaster but for peace. Your plans fill my future with hope.

⁓

Your Word says: "If I take the wings of the morning or live in the farthest part of the sea, even there Your hand will lead me and Your right hand will hold me" (Ps. 139:9–10 NLV).

I agree: No matter where I am, I am not too far from you. Your right hand holds my hand as you lead me.

⁓

Your Word says: "I will lead the blind by a way that they do not know. I will lead them in paths they do not know. I will turn darkness into light in front of them. And I will make the bad places smooth. These are the things I will do and I will not leave them" (Isa. 42:16 NLV).

I agree: When I can't see the way to go, you lead me down paths I did not find on my own. You cut through my darkness with your light so that I always know where to take my next step.

—

Your Word says: "Stand at the crossroads and look. Ask which paths are the old, reliable paths. Ask which way leads to blessings. Live that way, and find a resting place for yourselves" (Jer. 6:16 GW).

I agree: Lord, I am standing at the crossroads asking you for direction. I know you will point me to the reliable path and will show me the way that leads to blessings. You will show me how to follow you into rest.

—

Your Word says: "The heart of man plans his course, but ADONAI directs his steps" (Prov. 16:9 TLV).

I agree: Direct my steps even when I think I know which way to turn. Please keep me on your path.

—

Your Word says: "There are many plans in a man's heart, but it is the Lord's plan that will stand" (Prov. 19:21 NLV).

I agree: Though I have a lot of plans about what to do, you will guide me to your plans. Your plans will work out.

Your Word says: "If you do not have wisdom, ask God for it. He is always ready to give it to you and will never say you are wrong for asking" (James 1:5 NLV).

I agree: I am so glad that I can come to you for wisdom any time I need it. I'm asking you for wisdom now. Thank you that you will supply it.

Your Word says: "Christ gave you the Holy Spirit and He lives in you. You do not need anyone to teach you. The Holy Spirit is able to teach you all things. What He teaches you is truth and not a lie. Live by the help of Christ as the Holy Spirit has taught you" (1 John 2:27 NLV).

I agree: I have the Holy Spirit, who lives in me. He teaches me the truth in all things. I will live by Christ's help as the Spirit teaches me.

Your Word says: "Do not act like the sinful people of the world. Let God change your life. First of all, let Him give you a new mind. Then you will know what God wants you to do. And the things you do will be good and pleasing and perfect" (Rom. 12:2 NLV).

I agree: Change my life, Lord, so that I do not act in shameful ways. Give me a new mind so that I will know what you want me to do. And I will do good, pleasing, and perfect things.

Your Word says: "The fear of the LORD is the beginning of wisdom. The knowledge of the Holy One is understanding" (Prov. 9:10 GW).

I agree: Fearing you is the beginning of wisdom, and your Holy Spirit gives me understanding.

—

Your Word says: "For the Lord gives wisdom. Much learning and understanding come from His mouth. He stores up perfect wisdom for those who are right with Him. He is a safe-covering to those who are right in their walk. He watches over the right way, and He keeps safe the way of those who belong to Him. Then you will understand what is right and good, and right from wrong, and you will know what you should do. For wisdom will come into your heart. And much learning will be pleasing to your soul. Good thinking will keep you safe. Understanding will watch over you" (Prov. 2:6–11 NLV).

I agree: You give me wisdom, learning, and understanding because I am right with you. You are a safe covering because I am walking with you. You watch over me, leading me in the right way. Because I belong to you, you keep me safe. I will know what to do because your wisdom fills my heart so that I understand what is right and good as well as right from wrong. My soul is enriched when I study your Word. I will have good reasoning that will keep me safe. I will have understanding that will give me the insights I need.

—

Your Word says: "But we have the thoughts of Christ" (1 Cor. 2:16 NLV).

I agree: Thank you, Lord, that you give me your thoughts.

―

Dear Lord,

Thank you for these promises of direction for my life and decisions. I say yes and agree with them and believe they are for me. Give me even more faith to believe as I cling to your Word. I pray this in the power of the name of Jesus. Yes and amen.

9

Faith

But nothing is impossible for God.

Luke 1:37 GW

Sheila Walsh said, "We can trust a God who is holding the entire universe together to hold us together, even when everything is falling apart. He is the Creator of you and me; and He is also the sustainer of you and me."[1]

My friend Marilyn Turk can relate. She told me, "First, my mother died. Then my husband left. And finally the company where I'd worked twenty-five years was sold, and I lost my job."

That's a lot of stress, and Marilyn sought God. She prayed and trusted God to give her another job, quickly.

However, she wasn't hired for any of the jobs she applied for and found herself running out of money. She said, "Daily I prayed, asking God what I was doing wrong. Then in Matthew 6:33, I read, 'Seek the Kingdom of God above all else, and live righteously, and he will give you everything you need' (NLT).

"Without a job, I had time to join some Bible studies. Once I focused on God, I worried less about my needs, and God provided the job I needed at just the right time."[2]

We can have faith in a God we can trust. He is a God who comes through for us, though not always according to our schedule. Personally, I think he waits until we quit seeking our own solutions and finally realize that *he* is our solution.

If I had to describe our best gesture of faith, I would say it's simply trusting God.

Name above All Names

El Elyon means "the Most High God," and therefore, he is a God in whom we can put our trust.

Shadrach, Meshach, and Abednego were servants of *El Elyon* and got a glimpse of his identity the day they were thrown into the fiery furnace because they refused to worship the ninety-foot-tall golden image of King Nebuchadnezzar. The king was so angry with these Hebrews that he had his smelter heated seven times hotter than normal and threw the three men inside. But to the king's surprise, a fourth man appeared inside the furnace, shining like the Son of God.

The king called the three Hebrews out of the furnace and discovered that neither they nor their clothes had burned, and neither did they smell like smoke. The presence of God had done the impossible. God had protected the men from a rather heated situation.

Shadrach, Meshach, and Abednego trusted God with their very lives, and God moved on their behalf.

R. C. Sproul said, "It is one thing to believe in God—to believe that there is a God—and quite another thing to believe God. But living faith requires trusting the promise of God."[3]

Let's discover this living faith based on trust by touring the promise garden of faith.

THE PROMISE GARDEN OF FAITH

Your Word says: "If you have faith as a mustard seed, you will say to this mountain, 'Move from here to over there,' and it would move over. You will be able to do anything" (Matt. 17:20 NLV).

I agree: My faith may be as small as a mustard seed, but it is powerful. That's why I can say to the mountains of problems before me, "Move out of my way," and they will. I can do anything with and through you, God.

Your Word says: "I tell you, you can pray for anything, and if you believe that you've received it, it will be yours" (Mark 11:24 NLT).

I agree: I am praying, and I do believe that I will receive what I'm praying for.

Your Word says: "A man cannot please God unless he has faith. Anyone who comes to God must believe that He is. That one must also know that God gives what is promised to the one who keeps on looking for Him" (Heb. 11:6 NLV).

I agree: I cannot please you without faith. That's why I believe that you are the Most High God. You give me everything you promised because my focus is on you.

Your Word says: "Jesus said to him, 'As far as possibilities go, everything is possible for the person who believes'" (Mark 9:23 GW).

I agree: Jesus himself said that everything is possible if I believe. Lord, I do believe.

Your Word says: "But nothing is impossible for God" (Luke 1:37 GW).

I agree: Nothing is impossible for you, Lord.

Your Word says: "For sure, I tell you, whoever puts his trust in Me can do the things I am doing. He will do even greater things than these because I am going to the Father" (John 14:12 NLV).

I agree: Jesus, you said that if I put my trust in you, I can do not only the things you did but even greater things—because you are with the Father.

Your Word says: "Those who know Your name will put their trust in You. For You, O Lord, have never left alone those who look for You" (Ps. 9:10 NLV).

I agree: I look for you. I know your name and put my trust in you. You've never abandoned me.

Your Word says: "How happy is the man who has made the Lord his trust, and has not turned to the proud or to the followers of lies" (Ps. 40:4 NLV).

I agree: I am happy because I trust you, Lord. My trust in you keeps me from following those who are prideful or those who would deceive me.

Your Word says: "You will keep the man in perfect peace whose mind is kept on You, because he trusts in You. Trust in the Lord forever. For the Lord God is a Rock that lasts forever" (Isa. 26:3–4 NLV).

I agree: You keep me in perfect peace because my mind is focused on you, because I trust you. I will trust in you forever, for you are the Lord God, the rock that lasts forever.

Dear Lord,

Thank you for these promises regarding faith and our ability to trust you. I say yes and agree with them and believe they are for me. Give me even more faith to believe as I cling to your Word. I pray this in the power of the name of Jesus. Yes and amen.

10

Faithfulness of God

Who is like you, LORD God Almighty?
You, LORD, are mighty, and your faithfulness
surrounds you.

Psalm 89:8 NIV

R. C. Sproul said, "We break our promises to one another. We break
our promises to God. But God never breaks His promises to us."[1]

This is true because God is faithful.

In the book *Miracle on Hope Hill*, author Jennie Afman Dimkoff tells a story about how her pastor dad, in the days before cell
phones, had traveled a long way to visit a patient in a burn center.
After the visit, the pastor hoped he would have time to drop by his
now-empty home, a home that he and his wife were desperately
trying to sell. Despite the ads he'd placed in the paper, he'd had
no luck finding a buyer, and the house had become a financial
burden to his family.

After his hospital visit, the pastor was driving down the highway toward his old house when he realized he'd missed his exit. He decided to stop at a gas station to use the phone. But the phone booth was tied up by a man who was busy dialing phone number after phone number.

At first the pastor felt irritated, then he felt intrigued. Could the gentleman be looking to buy a house? The pastor bowed his head and prayed.

When the man finally emerged from the booth, he apologized for taking so long, but Pastor Afman held out his hand. "You wouldn't happen to be looking for a house to buy?" he inquired. "I happen to have one for sale in Durand."

Surprised, the man explained that he was looking to buy a home, and he wanted to buy one in Durand!

As it turned out, this man became the buyer of the pastor's house.[2]

How faithfully God answered the prayers of this pastor. Just think, Pastor Afman's wrong turn was actually the right turn, for God used it to meet the needs of his family. This story is an example of the promise found in the Psalms: "Your love, LORD, reaches to the heavens, your faithfulness to the skies" (36:5 NIV).

R. C. Sproul said, "Throughout history, God has demonstrated that He is supremely trustworthy. That's why in one sense, nothing could be more foolish than not to trust in the promises of God."[3]

Name above All Names

One of the names of God is *El Emunah*, "the faithful God." Deuteronomy 7:9 says, "Know therefore that the LORD your God is God; he is the faithful God, keeping his covenant of love to a thousand generations of those who love him and keep his commandments" (NIV). First Corinthians 1:9 says, "God faithfully keeps his promises" (GW).

How many times did God prove himself faithful to the people in the Bible who loved him? He faithfully helped David escape the jealous fits and murderous plots of King Saul. He closed the mouths of hungry lions when his servant Daniel had to spend the night in their den. He gave Sarah and Abraham the baby he'd promised them even though they were well past their childbearing years.

God is faithful not only to biblical greats but also to us.

Let's claim God's promises as we walk through the promise garden of the faithfulness of God.

The Promise Garden of the Faithfulness of God

Your Word says: "The loving-kindness of the Lord is given to the people of all times who honor Him" (Luke 1:50 NLV).

I agree: I honor you, Lord, and your loving-kindness is shining on me.

—

Your Word says: "God faithfully keeps his promises. He called you to be partners with his Son Jesus Christ our Lord" (1 Cor. 1:9 GW).

I agree: Lord, you are my promise keeper. You call me into partnership with your Son, my Lord Jesus Christ.

—

Your Word says: "But the Lord is faithful and will strengthen you and protect you against the evil one" (2 Thess. 3:3 GW).

I agree: How glad I am that you are faithful, Lord. You give me strength and protect me from the evil one.

Your Word says: "'Though the mountains be shaken and the hills be removed, yet my unfailing love for you will not be shaken nor my covenant of peace be removed,' says the LORD, who has compassion on you" (Isa. 54:10 NIV).

I agree: You have compassion on me. Though the mountains tremble and the hills melt away, your unfailing love for me will never be rocked, nor will you ever remove your covenant of peace from me.

Your Word says: "Because of the LORD's great love we are not consumed, for his compassions never fail. They are new every morning; great is your faithfulness" (Lam. 3:22–23 NIV).

I agree: Your faithfulness and love for me are great. Therefore, I will never be consumed. Your compassions toward me never fail and are fresh every morning.

Your Word says: "The LORD is merciful, compassionate, patient, and always ready to forgive" (Ps. 145:8 GW).

I agree: You are merciful, compassionate, and patient, and you always forgive me.

Your Word says: "Your love, LORD, reaches to the heavens, your faithfulness to the skies" (Ps. 36:5 NIV).

I agree: How wonderful to be loved by you, Lord; to know that your love for me reaches all the way to heaven and your faithfulness toward me is higher than the stars.

<hr>

Your Word says: "But the mercy of the LORD is from everlasting to everlasting upon them that fear him, and his righteousness unto children's children" (Ps. 103:17 KJV).

I agree: Because I honor and revere you, your mercy has no end. You count my children and me as righteous.

<hr>

Your Word says: "But you, Lord, are a compassionate and gracious God, slow to anger, abounding in love and faithfulness" (Ps. 86:15 NIV).

I agree: Lord, you are compassionate and gracious. You prove your love and faithfulness toward me with your enduring patience. Thank you.

<hr>

Your Word says: "Surely goodness and mercy shall follow me all the days of my life, and I shall dwell in the house of the LORD forever" (Ps. 23:6 ESV).

I agree: Your goodness and mercy follow me always and forever, and I will someday be with you in heaven.

Your Word says: "As high as the heavens are above the earth—that is how vast his mercy is toward those who fear him" (Ps. 103:11 GW).

I agree: I honor and revere you, Lord. Your mercy for me is higher than the heavens.

Dear Lord,

Thank you for these promises regarding your faithfulness. I say yes and agree with them and believe they are for me. Give me even more faith to believe as I cling to your Word. I pray this in the power of the name of Jesus. Yes and amen.

11

Godliness

For you died to this life, and your real life is hidden
with Christ in God.

Colossians 3:3 NLT

Author Julie Morris worried why she hadn't been able to lose
her harmful extra pounds and keep them off until she read John
15:4, where Jesus said, "Remain in me, as I also remain in you. No
branch can bear fruit by itself; it must remain in the vine. Neither
can you bear fruit unless you remain in me" (NIV).

Julie said, "I realized that he was telling me to stop being guided
by rigid diets and straining to produce willpower. Instead, he
wanted me to be guided by him and to trust him to produce in
me the spiritual fruit of self-control I so desperately needed."

With this new "diet advice" in mind, Julie couldn't wait to make
a list of practical ways to remain in him. She said, "As I made my
list, an exciting picture came into my mind: I saw myself, for the
first time, at a healthy weight!"

Her list of strategies included daily exploring the Bible for ways to remain in Jesus because she wanted to be guided into a healthier, more intimate relationship with him. She worked at not allowing herself to be distracted by resentments because, as she said, "Resentments are fattening!" She memorized Scripture promises to encourage healthy eating. Her favorite was Psalm 103:5, which says, "[He] satisfies your desires with good things so that your youth is renewed like the eagle's" (NIV). She also wrote prayers about her worries, casting them on the Lord (1 Pet. 5:7) instead of opening the refrigerator.

Julie said, "That was thirty-five years ago—the year I lost my weight! And I've kept it off too, because Jesus produced the spiritual fruit of self-control in me as I remained in him, one day at a time."[1]

Author Rhonda Kelley said, "Without self-control, we will be conformed to the world. With self-control, we will be conformed to the image of Christ (Rom. 12:12)."[2]

As we remain in Christ and are conformed to the image of Christ, we grow in godliness and in godly characteristics such as compassion, righteousness, loving-kindness, and self-control, the same characteristics found in God.

Name above All Names

Another precious name of God is *Elohei Chasdi*, which tells us that God is good, kind, and faithful. Psalm 136:1 describes God like this: "Give thanks to the LORD, for he is good. His love endures forever" (NIV).

We can see how good God is. He loved us so much that he wanted to restore our broken fellowship with him. So he sent his Son, who willingly took the punishment we deserved.

In the most agonizing moments of Jesus's earthly life, instead of focusing solely on his own pain, he had enough love to forgive the thief who was dying on the cross next to his.

So here's our picture of God: he is good, he is kind, and he is loving. When we realize what God has done for us and we desire to follow him, we will also want to be good, kind, and loving. That's what godliness is; it is becoming more like God.

The promises we will claim in the promise garden of godliness reveal how we can become more like the God who loves us.

THE PROMISE GARDEN OF GODLINESS

Your Word says: "Training the body helps a little, but godly living helps in every way. Godly living has the promise of life now and in the world to come" (1 Tim. 4:8 GW).

I agree: It's true that exercise helps to strengthen my body, but godly living helps to strengthen every part of my life and prepares me for the world to come.

—

Your Word says: "The LORD makes firm the steps of the one who delights in him; though he may stumble, he will not fall, for the LORD upholds him with his hand" (Ps. 37:23–24 NIV).

I agree: You, Lord, make my steps steady as I delight in you. Though I may stumble, I won't fall, for you hold my hand.

—

Your Word says: "Seek the Kingdom of God above all else, and he will give you everything you need" (Luke 12:31 NLT).

I agree: Lord, I want to seek your kingdom above everything else. Thank you for giving me all that I need.

Your Word says: "Whoever is a believer in Christ is a new creation. The old way of living has disappeared. A new way of living has come into existence" (2 Cor. 5:17 GW).

I agree: I am a new creation because I believe in Christ. My old ways of living have been replaced with new ways that reflect my life in Christ.

Your Word says: "Remain in me, as I also remain in you. No branch can bear fruit by itself; it must remain in the vine. Neither can you bear fruit unless you remain in me" (John 15:4 NIV).

I agree: I remain in you, Lord, and you remain in me. Fruit does not grow unless it's attached to the vine. I want to be fruitful, and so I will stay attached to you.

Your Word says: "And if anyone gives even a cup of cold water to one of these little ones who is my disciple, truly I tell you, that person will certainly not lose their reward" (Matt. 10:42 NIV).

I agree: Lord, show me how to bless those who belong to you. When I do, I will certainly not lose my reward.

Your Word says: "Blessed are the merciful, for they shall receive mercy" (Matt. 5:7 ESV).

I agree: Help me to be merciful to others, Lord, as you are merciful to me.

Your Word says: "Therefore, since we have these promises, dear friends, let us purify ourselves from everything that contaminates body and spirit, perfecting holiness out of reverence for God" (2 Cor. 7:1 NIV).

I agree: Help me to purify myself from any sin that would contaminate my body and spirit. I want to practice holiness out of my reverence for you.

Your Word says: "Through these he has given us his very great and precious promises, so that through them you may participate in the divine nature, having escaped the corruption in the world caused by evil desires" (2 Pet. 1:4 NIV).

I agree: Lord, through your wonderful and precious promises, I can enjoy your divine nature and escape evil desires that lead to corruption.

Your Word says: "There isn't any temptation that you have experienced which is unusual for humans. God, who faithfully keeps his promises, will not allow you to be tempted beyond your power to resist. But when you are tempted, he will also give you the ability to endure the temptation as your way of escape" (1 Cor. 10:13 GW).

I agree: I have not experienced any temptations that are unusual. But I serve you, Lord, a God who keeps his promises. You will give me the power to escape every temptation so that I will have the power to escape sin.

Your Word says: "I can do everything through Christ who strengthens me" (Phil. 4:13 GW).

I agree: I am strong because I can do everything though Christ who gives me strength.

Your Word says: "Therefore, I urge you, brothers and sisters, in view of God's mercy, to offer your bodies as a living sacrifice, holy and pleasing to God—this is your true and proper worship. Do not conform to the pattern of this world, but be transformed by the renewing of your mind. Then you will be able to test and approve what God's will is—his good, pleasing and perfect will" (Rom. 12:1–2 NIV).

I agree: I will present you with true and honoring worship as I offer you my body as a living sacrifice. In this way, I can be holy and pleasing to you. I also promise to steer clear of the pattern of this world. Transform me by renewing my mind in you. Then I will be able to find and follow your will for me.

Dear Lord,

Thank you for these promises concerning godliness. I say yes and agree with them and believe they are for me. Give me even more faith to believe as I cling to your Word. I pray this in the power of the name of Jesus. Yes and amen.

12

Healing

"I'll restore your health and heal your wounds," declares the LORD.

Jeremiah 30:17 GW

Do God's promises apply to healing? Andrew Murray, the turn-of-the-century pastor who inspired so many students at Moody Bible Institute, thought so. That was especially true after God healed him of a two-year illness. Murray explained that he was healed "by the mercy of God in answer to the prayer of those who see him as *the Lord Thy Healer* (Exodus 15:26)."[1]

Because of his healing, Murray decided he could no longer be silent on the issue of healing and published a series of meditations about the prayer of faith, which he described as "the means appointed by God for the cure of the sick."[2] In these writings, Murray explained, "Jesus came to deliver men from sin and sickness that He might make known the love of the Father."[3]

You might be thinking, *The apostles were able to heal, and maybe healing worked for beloved pastors at the turn of the century, but what about today? Does God still heal today?*

My friend Carol Graham has seen God heal numerous times. She told me, "One Sunday morning during my visit at a church, the minister announced that their youth pastor, who had a young son and a pregnant wife, was in the hospital dying. He said that anyone who wanted to say good-bye to him should do so, as this young man was so filled with cancer that he was not expected to live through the night."

Carol said, "The Lord prompted me to go pray for him. I argued that it wasn't my place, yet I knew I had to be obedient. So boldly, yet nervously, I walked into the ICU where twenty-five friends and family members were crying in the lounge area.

"My feet felt like lead, and I wanted to run away. But with each step I took toward the family, I became bolder. After I asked for permission to pray, the family discussed it and then reluctantly agreed, but they asked to be present.

"I walked up to the dying man, took his limp hand in mine, and whispered, 'The Spirit of him that raised up Jesus from the dead dwells in you and shall quicken your mortal body' [see Rom. 8:11 KJV]. After I said this, his eyelids fluttered. I repeated this Scripture passage five times. Each time the man responded with more strength until he was sitting up in bed.

"Everyone in the room was gasping as they watched this miracle unfold before their eyes. I told them, 'He will be with you in church next Sunday.' And he was."[4]

Could it be that some of us have been missing the truth that God still heals today?

Maybe you're still not convinced. Perhaps you've had a bad experience. Maybe you've prayed for the sick and not seen the results you'd hoped for. Me too. But that doesn't mean I'm going to stop believing that God can heal. Maybe I blew it, or maybe God was healing through the transformation of death to eternal life. I don't know. But I do know this. I've also seen God heal the sick. Recently, I saw a woman who was scheduled for hip surgery within the week. My friends and I prayed for her, and God instantly healed her hip, and she went home and canceled her surgery.

Just last week I prayed for a man who didn't yet understand that God's grace was for him, and God instantly healed his painful shoulder. In that instant, his eyes opened wide to the understanding that God loved him.

Andrew Murray cautioned, "Christian who is sick, if you really seek to know what is the will of God in this thing, don't let yourself be influenced by the opinion of others or by your own former ideas, but listen to and study what the word of God has to say."[5]

Name above All Names

One of God's many names is *Jehovah Rapha*, which means "the Lord who heals you." God told Moses and his people, "If you will listen carefully to the LORD your God and do what he considers right, if you pay attention to his commands and obey all his laws, I will never make you suffer any of the diseases I made the Egyptians suffer, because I am the LORD, who heals you" (Exod. 15:26 GW).

Luke 9:1–2 says, "Jesus called the twelve apostles together and gave them power and authority over every demon and power and authority to cure diseases. He sent them to spread the message about God's kingdom and to cure the sick" (GW). Then in verse 6 we read, "The apostles went from village to village, told the Good News, and cured the sick everywhere" (GW).

The power and authority of Jesus are more powerful than we can possibly imagine. When we add this power into our lives and combine it with the power of God's promises, miracles can result, especially concerning:

- addiction
- energy
- a long life
- a sound mind

Let's take a trip to the promise garden of healing to find out what these promises are all about.

THE PROMISE GARDEN OF HEALING

Your Word says: "The Holy Spirit raised Jesus from the dead. If the same Holy Spirit lives in you, He will give life to your bodies in the same way" (Rom. 8:11 NLV).

I agree: The Holy Spirit is the power and the force that raised Jesus from the dead, and he also lives in me. He gives life to my body in much the same way that he raised Jesus from the dead.

***

Your Word says: "His wounds have healed you!" (1 Pet. 2:24 NLV).

I agree: By your wounds, I am healed.

***

Your Word says: "Praise the LORD, my soul, and never forget all the good he has done: He is the one who forgives all your sins, the one who heals all your diseases" (Ps. 103:2–3 GW).

I agree: With gladness I praise you, Lord, and never forget the good you have done. You forgive all my sins and heal all my diseases.

—

Your Word says: "'I'll restore your health and heal your wounds,' declares the LORD" (Jer. 30:17 GW).

I agree: Lord, you promised to restore my health and heal my wounds.

—

Your Word says: "Heal me, O Lord, and I will be healed. Save me and I will be saved. For You are my praise" (Jer. 17:14 NLV).

I agree: Lord, you are the one I praise. When you heal me, I am healed. When you save me, I am saved.

—

Your Word says: "Is anyone among you sick? Let them call the elders of the church to pray over them and anoint them with oil in the name of the Lord. And the prayer offered in faith will make the sick person well; the Lord will raise them up. If they have sinned, they will be forgiven" (James 5:14–15 NIV).

I agree: I will anoint the sick with oil and call upon the name of the Lord to heal. My prayers of faith will make the sick person well, and God will raise them up and forgive their sins.

Your Word says: "O LORD my God, I cried out to you for help, and you healed me" (Ps. 30:2 GW).

I agree: Lord, what joy! You helped me and healed me!

Your Word says: "I am the LORD, who heals you" (Exod. 15:26 GW).

I agree: Lord, you are my healer!

Your Word says: "Tell your sins to each other. And pray for each other so you may be healed. The prayer from the heart of a man right with God has much power" (James 5:16 NLV).

I agree: Because I know that a righteous person's prayers have much power, I will push into righteousness by confessing my sins to fellow believers. Then when we pray for one another, we will be healed.

ADDICTION

Your Word says: "Children, you belong to God, and you have defeated these enemies. God's Spirit is in you and is more powerful than the one that is in the world" (1 John 4:4 CEV).

I agree: God, you have defeated my enemies, and I belong to you. Your Spirit is in me and is more powerful than the spirit of the evil one. You can defeat my every addiction.

—

Your Word says: "But if God's Spirit lives in you, you are under the control of your spiritual nature, not your corrupt nature" (Rom. 8:9 GW).

I agree: Because I belong to Christ, your Spirit lives in me and I am under the Spirit's control. I will no longer allow my flesh to dictate my actions but will do what the Holy Spirit instructs.

—

Your Word says: "Every child of God can defeat the world, and our faith is what gives us this victory. No one can defeat the world without having faith in Jesus as the Son of God" (1 John 5:4–5 CEV).

I agree: I am your child, and that means I can defeat the world. It is my faith in you, Lord, that gives me every victory. I would never be able to defeat the world if I had not placed my faith in Christ Jesus.

ENERGY

Your Word says: "He gives strength to the weak. And He gives power to him who has little strength. Even very young men get tired and become weak and strong young men trip and fall. But they who wait upon the Lord will get new strength. They will rise up with wings like eagles. They will run and not get tired. They will walk and not become weak" (Isa. 40:29–31 NLV).

I agree: Lord, you give me strength when I am weak. Even the strong get tired, but when I seek you, Lord, you renew my strength so I can soar like eagles. I will run and not grow tired. I will walk and not become weak.

—

Your Word says: "We have this light from God in our human bodies. This shows that the power is from God. It is not from ourselves" (2 Cor. 4:7 NLV).

I agree: I have your living light inside my body, Lord. This is your power, not mine.

—

Your Word says: "I can do everything through Christ who strengthens me" (Phil. 4:13 GW).

I agree: I can do anything through Jesus Christ because he strengthens me.

—

Your Word says: "Those who feel tired and worn out will find new life and energy" (Jer. 31:25 CEV).

I agree: When I am tired and worn out, you will give me new life and energy.

—

Your Word says: "'Not by strength nor by power, but by My Spirit,' says the Lord of All" (Zech. 4:6 NLV).

I agree: Lord, my strength, abilities, and callings are not based on my power but on the power of the Holy Spirit.

—

Your Word says: "I'm asking God to give you a gift from the wealth of his glory. I pray that he would give you inner strength and power through his Spirit" (Eph. 3:16 GW).

I agree: I receive your gift of glory so that my inner strength will be renewed through the power of your Spirit.

A LONG LIFE

Your Word says: "My son, do not forget my teaching. Let your heart keep my words. For they will add to you many days and years of life and peace" (Prov. 3:1–2 NLV).

I agree: I will listen to your Word and keep it, for your words and promises will add many days and even years to my peaceful life.

—

Your Word says: "With long life I will satisfy him and show him my salvation" (Ps. 91:16 NIV).

I agree: Bless your name! You satisfy me with long life and show me your salvation.

—

Your Word says: "Walk in obedience to all that the LORD your God has commanded you, so that you may live and prosper and prolong your days in the land that you will possess" (Deut. 5:33 NIV).

I agree: Lord, I will follow you in obedience so that I may live, prosper, and prolong my days in this life you have given me.

—

Your Word says: "Honor your father and your mother, that your days may be long upon the land which the Lord your God is giving you" (Exod. 20:12 NKJV).

I agree: I will honor my father and mother so that my days will be many.

A SOUND MIND

Your Word says: "For God did not give us a spirit of fear. He gave us a spirit of power and of love and of a good mind" (2 Tim. 1:7 NLV).

I agree: Lord, you are not the one who puts fear in me. Instead, you give me a spirit of power, love, and a good, strong mind.

—

Your Word says: "We break down every thought and proud thing that puts itself up against the wisdom of God. We take hold of every thought and make it obey Christ" (2 Cor. 10:5 NLV).

I agree: I pull down thoughts and my own pride, which try to block your wisdom. I take hold of every thought and make it bow before Christ.

—

Your Word says: "Don't copy the behavior and customs of this world, but let God transform you into a new person by changing the way you think. Then you will learn to know God's will for you, which is good and pleasing and perfect" (Rom. 12:2 NLT).

I agree: Lord, I won't copy those in the world but will let you transform me into a new person, with your thoughts. That is how I will know your good and perfect will for me.

―

Your Word says: "Without counsel plans fail, but with many advisers they succeed" (Prov. 15:22 ESV).

I agree: My plans may fail unless I follow wise counsel. Good advisers will bring me success.

―

Your Word says: "There is no fear in love. Perfect love puts fear out of our hearts" (1 John 4:18 NLV).

I agree: Love has no hidden fears, and perfect love draws fear from my heart.

―

Your Word says: "'Who can know the LORD's thoughts? Who knows enough to teach him?' But we understand these things, for we have the mind of Christ" (1 Cor. 2:16 NLT).

I agree: You, Lord, do not need to be schooled by me, nor am I wise enough to understand your thoughts. However, you give me understanding because I have the mind of Christ.

—

Dear Lord,

Thank you for these promises regarding healing, addiction, energy, a long life, and a sound mind. I say yes and agree with them and believe they are for me. Give me even more faith to believe as I cling to your Word. I pray this in the power of the name of Jesus. Yes and amen.

13

Heaven

And this world is fading away, along with everything
that people crave. But anyone who does what pleases
God will live forever.

1 John 2:17 NLT

Don Piper, the author of *90 Minutes in Heaven*, said, "Experiencing Heaven is the most real thing that's ever happened to me. I did
not want to come back. If you've ever been there, you don't want
to be here. But when I did come back here, I intensified my efforts
exponentially to help people understand the free gift of Heaven
offered through Christ."[1]

I love Don's testimony, especially now that I have beloved family members in heaven. And I have to admit, heaven seems closer
to me now than ever before. The fact is it's really only a single
heartbeat, a mere breath, away.

My understanding of heaven grew when, last summer, I held
my disabled daughter's hand for the last time. I'd decided not to

fight her coming death, as I could no longer deny her heaven. In the past, whenever we'd talk about heaven, I would tease her by saying, "One day it will be your turn to go, but not today." But on this day, I told her, "Laura, today *is* your turn."

In her last hours, with her dad, her brother, and me gathered around her, she clung to our every word. We each told her how much we loved her, and then I began to read God's promises to her. I shared promises about God's love, promises about her own salvation, and then as she was nearing the end, promises about heaven.

Her eyes gleamed as I shared these words of Jesus: "My Father's house has many rooms; if that were not so, would I have told you that I am going there to prepare a place for you? And if I go and prepare a place for you, I will come back and take you to be with me that you also may be where I am. You know the way to the place where I am going" (John 14:2–4 NIV).

I told her, "Laura, you are going to heaven today. Your grand-dad can't wait to see you. Jesus is so excited that you are coming. He's sent an angel to give you safe passage."

At that very moment, Laura smiled and slipped from her body into the waiting arms of Christ.

As I look back on that scene, I am so happy that I could share the promises of salvation and heaven with my daughter, giving her the confidence to let go and allow God to transform her into her heavenly self.

Name above All Names

One of God's names, *Adonai Tzva'ot*, means "the Lord of hosts" or "the Lord of the armies of heaven." This was the very name David called out before killing the giant Goliath with his slingshot and a single stone: "You are coming to me with a sword, a spear and a javelin, but I am coming to you in the Name of Adonai-*Tzva'ot*, God of the armies of Israel, whom you have defied" (1 Sam. 17:45 TLV).

Our God is the leader of the heavenly armies, as seen by Elisha the prophet and his young servant. They were in trouble with King Aram because Elisha had leaked Aram's secret plans, revealed by God himself, to the King of Israel. So King Aram sent an army to capture the prophet. Imagine Elisha's servant walking out into the morning only to discover the army of Aram surrounding them. He ran for Elisha, who took the sight of Aram's army in stride. Elisha prayed to the Lord of heaven, the Lord of the heavenly hosts, to open the eyes of his servant so he could see.

That's when the young man saw that the hillside around them was filled with horses and chariots of fire. "'Don't be afraid!' Elisha told him, 'For there are more on our side than on theirs!'" (2 Kings 6:16 NLT).

And so this decree remains true to this day. Heaven's hosts outnumber our enemy, and our God is the leader of that heavenly army.

It's time we explore what the promises of heaven are all about. In addition to verses about heaven itself, we will discover verses about:

- the assurance of heaven
- death in Christ
- eternal life

THE PROMISE GARDEN OF HEAVEN

Your Word says: "My Father's house has many rooms; if that were not so, would I have told you that I am going there to prepare a place for you? And if I go and prepare a place for you, I will come back and take you to be with me that you also may be where I am. You know the way to the place where I am going" (John 14:2–4 NIV).

I agree: You, dear Lord, have many rooms in your house. And to think that Jesus is already preparing one of those rooms for me. One day Jesus himself will take me there so I can be with him forever.

Your Word says: "'He will wipe every tear from their eyes. There will be no more death or mourning or crying or pain, for the old order of things has passed away.' He who was seated on the throne said, 'I am making everything new!' Then he said, 'Write this down, for these words are trustworthy and true.' He said to me: 'It is done. I am the Alpha and the Omega, the Beginning and the End. To the thirsty I will give water without cost from the spring of the water of life. Those who are victorious will inherit all this, and I will be their God and they will be my children'" (Rev. 21:4–7 NIV).

I agree: In heaven, you will wipe away my tears, and there will be no more death or pain. All my earthly woes will have passed away because you are making all things new. You are the Alpha and the Omega, the Beginning and the End. You will give me water from the spring of life without charge. I am victorious and will inherit all this from you. You are my God, and I am your child.

Your Word says: "There will no longer be any curse. The throne of God and the lamb will be in the city. His servants will worship him and see his face. His name will be on their foreheads. There will be no more night, and they will not need any light from lamps or the sun because the Lord God will shine on them. They will rule as kings forever and ever. He said to me, 'These words are trustworthy and true. The Lord God of the spirits of the prophets has sent his angel to show his servants the things that must happen soon. I'm coming soon! Blessed is the one who follows the words of the prophecy in this book'" (Rev. 22:3–7 GW).

I agree: In heaven, there will be no curse. Your throne and the lamb of God will be there. I will worship you and see your face. Your name will be on my forehead. Heaven will be as bright as day because of your glory. You are the Lord, and you are coming soon. I am blessed to have your word on this.

THE ASSURANCE OF HEAVEN

Your Word says: "My sheep hear My voice and I know them. They follow Me. I give them life that lasts forever. They will never be punished. No one is able to take them out of My hand. My Father Who gave them to Me is greater than all. No one is able to take them out of My Father's hand" (John 10:27–29 NLV).

I agree: Jesus, I hear your voice and follow you, for you are the one who gives me life that lasts forever. I will not be punished because the Father gave me to you. No one can take me out of your hand or the hand of the Father.

Your Word says: "I know the One in Whom I have put my trust. I am sure He is able to keep safe that which I have trusted to Him until the day He comes again" (2 Tim. 1:12 NLV).

I agree: How wonderful that I can put my full trust in you. You will keep me safe because I have been entrusted to you.

⁓

Your Word says: "For I know that nothing can keep us from the love of God. Death cannot! Life cannot! Angels cannot! Leaders cannot! Any other power cannot! Hard things now or in the future cannot! The world above or the world below cannot! Any other living thing cannot keep us away from the love of God which is ours through Christ Jesus our Lord" (Rom. 8:38–39 NLV).

I agree: Nothing can keep me from your love, dear God, including death, life, angels, leaders, any other power, or even difficulties present or to come. Because your love is mine through Christ Jesus my Lord, not even the world below or any living thing can take your love from me.

⁓

Your Word says: "Jesus said to her, 'I am the One Who raises the dead and gives them life. Anyone who puts his trust in Me will live again, even if he dies. Anyone who lives and has put his trust in Me will never die. Do you believe this?'" (John 11:25–26 NLV)

I agree: You raise the dead and give them life. I put my trust in you, and so even if I die, I will live again. I believe—in fact, I know—that I will never die.

DEATH IN CHRIST

Your Word says: "So we are always confident. We know that as long as we are living in these bodies, we are living away from the

Lord. Indeed, our lives are guided by faith, not by sight. We are confident and prefer to live away from this body and to live with the Lord" (2 Cor. 5:6–8 GW).

I agree: Lord, I am not yet with you in heaven, as I am still living in my body. So while I am still here on earth, my life is guided by faith, not by sight. But one day I will leave my body, and you will receive me into heaven. Oh, what a glad day that will be!

⌁

Your Word says: "I heard a loud voice from the throne say, 'God lives with humans! God will make his home with them, and they will be his people. God himself will be with them and be their God. He will wipe every tear from their eyes. There won't be any more death. There won't be any grief, crying, or pain, because the first things have disappeared'" (Rev. 21:3–4 GW).

I agree: You live with me. You make your home with me, and I belong to you. You are my God. When I enter heaven's gates, you will wipe every tear from my eyes, and death will be no more. There will be no more grief, crying, or pain, as those things will have faded away.

ETERNAL LIFE

Your Word says: "And this world is fading away, along with everything that people crave. But anyone who does what pleases God will live forever" (1 John 2:17 NLT).

I agree: This world is fading away, including all that I crave. But if I do what pleases you, I will live forever.

Your Word says: "You get what is coming to you when you sin. It is death! But God's free gift is life that lasts forever. It is given to us by our Lord Jesus Christ" (Rom. 6:23 NLV).

I agree: Sin gives me death. But your wonderful, free gift of life lasts forever and is given to me by my Lord Jesus Christ.

Your Word says: "For God so loved the world that He gave His only Son. Whoever puts his trust in God's Son will not be lost but will have life that lasts forever" (John 3:16 NLV).

I agree: God, you loved the world, so you gave your Son Jesus. When I put my trust in your Son, I will not be lost but will live forever.

Your Word says: "God gave us life that lasts forever, and this life is in His Son. He that has the Son has life. He that does not have the Son of God does not have life" (1 John 5:11–12 NLV).

I agree: You gave me life that lasts forever, and this life is in Jesus. I have Jesus, so I have life.

Dear Lord,

Thank you for these promises regarding heaven. I say yes and agree with them and believe they are for me. Give me even more faith to believe as I cling to your Word. I pray this in the power of the name of Jesus. Yes and amen.

14

Hope

> I have told you these things so you may have peace in
> Me. In the world you will have much trouble. But take
> hope! I have power over the world!
>
> John 16:33 NLV

Anne Graham Lotz, in her book *God's Story*, said, "When you find yourself drowning in overwhelming circumstances, ask God to give you a promise to which you can cling—a promise on which you can base your hope."[1]

My friend Janet Perez Eckles discovered such a promise in Deuteronomy 31:8: "Do not be afraid or discouraged, for the LORD will personally go ahead of you. He will be with you; he will neither fail you nor abandon you" (NLT).

Janet explained that some years ago, while her three little boys played in the family room, she sat on her unmade bed clutching a wrinkled tissue and asking God why he was punishing her. In a matter of eighteen months, a retinal disease had robbed her of her sight. Her husband had been traumatized by her sudden blindness and had announced he couldn't stay.

She said, "Loneliness added to my hopelessness and fear. They nagged me night and day. Not only was I facing complete physical blindness, but I had also become spiritually blind to God's Word. But when I called out to him, God opened the eyes of my heart so I could see his reassurance in his Word."

In the quietness of her heart, God spoke to her. He told her not to be afraid. He told her that he would go with her in her darkness, and even if her husband left her, she'd never be alone. Janet said, "This reassurance shined the light of hope and cast a sweet ray of peace that eventually turned to joy."

Her marriage healed, and she was able to continue to be a mom to her kids. Plus, as she explained, "I now had the security that God would always be by my side."[2]

Janet is one of my heroes. She travels the world, by herself, to share the hope of Jesus with groups across the United States and South America. But as she will tell you, she's never alone. Not only is God with her, but he also always sends the right person at the right time to help her get to where she needs to go. He has never disappointed her hope in him.

Janet's story reminds me of these words of Corrie ten Boom: "Never be afraid to trust an unknown future to a known God."[3]

Praise be to him! God is known to us. He is our God of hope!

Name above All Names

Another name for God is *Adonai*, which means that God is our Lord and Master, the great God in whom we can hope. In Jeremiah 29:11, the Tree of Life Version of the Bible explains his thoughts toward us this way: "'For I know the plans that I have in mind for you,' declares ADONAI, 'plans for *shalom* and not calamity—to give you a future and a hope.'"

Let's look at how a desperate Hebrew psalmist described his hope in *Adonai* in Psalm 130:

> I wait for ADONAI, my soul waits,
> and in His word I hope.
> My soul waits for my Lord,
> more than watchmen for the morning,
> watchmen for the morning. (vv. 5–6 TLV)

Isn't that what hoping in the Lord is about? It's about waiting on God, having faith that he will move on our behalf.

Let's explore the promise garden of hope for promises that will inspire our faith while we wait in hope for our *Adonai* to move on our behalf.

THE PROMISE GARDEN OF HOPE

Your Word says: "I have told you these things so you may have peace in Me. In the world you will have much trouble. But take hope! I have power over the world" (John 16:33 NLV).

I agree: I have peace in you because of your promises to me. I have hope even when I have trouble in this world, for you, Lord, have power over the world.

⁓

Your Word says: "No, the LORD's delight is in those who fear him, those who put their hope in his unfailing love" (Ps. 147:11 NLT).

I agree: You delight in me because I honor and revere you and because I gladly put my hope in your unfailing love.

Your Word says: "I know the plans that I have for you, declares the LORD. They are plans for peace and not disaster, plans to give you a future filled with hope" (Jer. 29:11 GW).

I agree: I trust your plans for me, Lord. Your plans are for peace, not disaster. You gift me with a future filled with hope.

Your Word says: "Blessed be the God and Father of our Lord *Yeshua* the Messiah! In His great mercy He caused us to be born again to a living hope through the resurrection of Messiah *Yeshua* from the dead" (1 Pet. 1:3 TLV).

I agree: Blessed are you, Lord, the Father of my Jesus! You've shown great mercy to me. You caused me to be born again to a living hope through the resurrection of Jesus from the dead.

Your Word says: "May the God of hope fill you with all joy and peace as you trust in him, so that you may overflow with hope by the power of the Holy Spirit" (Rom. 15:13 NIV).

I agree: Lord of hope, fill me with more joy and peace as I trust you so that I may overflow with hope by the power of the Holy Spirit.

Your Word says: "Behold, I am coming soon" (Rev. 22:12 TLV).

I agree: Yes! My hope is in you. You are coming soon.

Your Word says: "We are hunted down, but never abandoned by God. We get knocked down, but we are not destroyed" (2 Cor. 4:9 NLT).

I agree: Lord, when I am stalked by the enemy, you are with me; you never leave my side. When I am knocked to my knees, I hope in you, and I am never destroyed.

Your Word says: "Do not be afraid or discouraged, for the LORD will personally go ahead of you. He will be with you; he will neither fail you nor abandon you" (Deut. 31:8 NLT).

I agree: Why be afraid or discouraged? Lord, you go before me. You are always with me, and you will never fail or abandon me.

Your Word says: "The Lord is near to all who call on Him, to all who call on Him in truth" (Ps. 145:18 NLV).

I agree: Lord, I am calling out to you in truth. I know you are near!

Your Word says: "The Lord is my light and the One Who saves me. Whom should I fear? The Lord is the strength of my life. Of whom should I be afraid?" (Ps. 27:1 NLV)

I agree: You, Lord, are my light and the one who saves me. You are my strength. I do not need to be afraid of anyone because when I am in your strength, there is no one I need to fear.

Your Word says: "The Lord holds up all who fall. He raises up all who are brought down" (Ps. 145:14 NLV).

I agree: Lord, when I fall, you pick me up. You raise me up whenever I hit the ground.

Your Word says: "The LORD directs the steps of the godly. He delights in every detail of their lives. Though they stumble, they will never fall, for the LORD holds them by the hand" (Ps. 37:23–24 NLT).

I agree: You are interested in me as well as in the smallest details of my life. You not only direct my steps but also hold my hand so that if I stumble, I will not fall.

Your Word says: "He lifted me out of the pit of despair, out of the mud and the mire. He set my feet on solid ground and steadied me as I walked along. He has given me a new song to sing, a hymn of praise to our God. Many will see what he has done and be amazed" (Ps. 40:2–3 NLT).

I agree: I praise you! You lifted me out of my despair and placed my feet on solid ground. You held me steady throughout my life's journey. You've given me a new song to sing praises to you. Many will see what you have done for me and will be amazed.

Your Word says: "My dear children, I'm writing this to you so that you will not sin. Yet, if anyone does sin, we have Jesus Christ, who has God's full approval. He speaks on our behalf when we come into the presence of the Father. He is the payment for our sins, and not only for our sins, but also for the sins of the whole world" (1 John 2:1–2 GW).

I agree: I am your dear child. You have let me know that it is your wish that I not sin. But if I do, you have given me grace and forgiveness through Jesus Christ, the one who lived a perfect life. He died in my place. He speaks up for me when I come into your presence, Lord. He died on the cross, not just for my sins but for the sins of everyone.

Your Word says: "Great is his faithfulness; his mercies begin afresh each morning" (Lam. 3:23 NLT).

I agree: Great is your faithfulness. I love how your mercies are new every morning!

Dear Lord,

Thank you for these promises regarding hope. I say yes and agree with them and believe they are for me. Give me even more faith to believe as I cling to your Word. I pray this in the power of the name of Jesus. Yes and amen.

15

Joy

Do not be sad for the joy of the Lord is your strength.

Nehemiah 8:10 NLV

Though my daughter doesn't live on this earth anymore, it's a comfort to know that she lives in heaven.

Learning how to live without her has not been easy. My home, once a vibrant place of community surrounding Laura's care, is now much too quiet.

Then there's the issue of my rage. You see, shortly before Laura died, an order was changed without our approval. So instead of taking my daughter home from the hospital, as we'd thought, we'd held her funeral.

So not only was I dealing with grief, I was also dealing with betrayal and white-hot anger.

My anger wasn't wrong, because what happened to my daughter *was* wrong. But I had to make a choice to live in grief and rage or to not.

I think the biggest part of my emotional recovery came when God's Spirit whispered to my heart, *Give it all to me.* And with his help, I did.

No, I will never condone what happened to my daughter, but now this problem belongs to God to resolve however he likes. He does not need my help.

Looking back, I can tell you that when I let go of my grief and anger, something incredible happened. I was suddenly flooded with God's supernatural joy and peace.

I miss my daughter, yes. I really do. But I know she is with God, and I know God is with me too. And now that my joy has returned, so has my strength to continue in the call he has for my life.

In case you haven't heard, joy is not about your circumstances. It's more about trusting God no matter your circumstances. In her book *Pure Joy*, Alicia Britt Chole said, "In David's time, the hope of many rested on the outcome of the year's harvest. If the crops were plentiful, the community rejoiced. If the crops failed, the community despaired. But David experienced a joy that flourished even when the crops perished. He treasured a joy that thrived even through the drought. David knew a joy that was pure. Such joy flows from one source: the living God."[1]

Charles Swindoll explained joy in difficult circumstances this way: "A half-dozen joy stealers may be waiting outside your door, ready to pounce at the first opportunity. However, nothing can rob you of your hold on grace, your claim to peace, or your confidence in God without your permission. Choose joy. Never release your grip."[2]

Name above All Names

Imagine serving a God whose name means "God my exceeding joy." One of God's names, *El Simchath Gili*, means exactly that.

As the apostle Paul said, "May God, the source of hope, fill you with joy and peace through your faith in him" (Rom. 15:13 GW).

Nehemiah, the Hebrew cupbearer of King Artaxerxes, got permission to return to Jerusalem a hundred years after King Nebuchadnezzar had sacked it. He and the men worked to rebuild the ruined walls. When the work was done, Nehemiah had another task to complete. His people had lived their entire lives in captivity and had lost not only their identity but also their knowledge of God.

Nehemiah called an assembly so that he could read the law of Moses to them. The people, upon discovering that they belonged to God, began to weep. Nehemiah told them, "Do not grieve, for the joy of the LORD is your strength" (Neh. 8:10 NIV).

What glorious words! The joy of the Lord is our strength too.

Let's explore the promise garden of joy so that we can declare our joy unto the Lord as well.

THE PROMISE GARDEN OF JOY

Your Word says: "Do not be sad for the joy of the Lord is your strength" (Neh. 8:10 NLV).

I agree: I have no reason to be sad. The joy of the Lord is my strength!

Your Word says: "Be full of joy always because you belong to the Lord. Again I say, be full of joy" (Phil. 4:4 NLV).

I agree: Joy is mine! I choose to be joyful because I belong to you, Lord.

Your Word says: "Even if the fig tree does not grow figs and there is no fruit on the vines, even if the olives do not grow and the fields give no food, even if there are no sheep within the fence and no cattle in the cattle-building, yet I will have joy in the Lord. I will be glad in the God Who saves me" (Hab. 3:17–18 NLV).

I agree: If I encounter loss or my plans rot or my dreams fail, or even if there is no money in my checking account to pay my bills, I will be joyful in you, Lord, because you are the God who rescues me.

Your Word says: "For his anger lasts only a moment, but his favor lasts a lifetime! Weeping may last through the night, but joy comes with the morning" (Ps. 30:5 NLT).

I agree: How happy I am that your anger is fleeting and does not compare to the lifetime of favor you've planned for me. I may weep through the night, but I will encounter joy in the morning.

Your Word says: "I have told you these things so My joy may be in you and your joy may be full" (John 15:11 NLV).

I agree: Thank you for sharing your promise with me so that your joy will be in me. This joy is complete.

Your Word says: "For the Kingdom of God is not a matter of what we eat or drink, but of living a life of goodness and peace and joy in the Holy Spirit" (Rom. 14:17 NLT).

I agree: The good news is that the kingdom of God is about living a life of goodness, peace, and joy in the Holy Spirit.

Dear Lord,

Thank you for these promises regarding joy. I say yes and agree with them and believe they are for me. Give me even more faith to believe as I cling to your Word. I pray this in the power of the name of Jesus. Yes and amen.

16

Love

See how very much our Father loves us, for he calls us
his children, and that is what we are!

1 John 3:1 NLT

Billy Graham, in *Peace with God*, said, "Never question God's
great love, for it is as unchangeable a part of God as is His holiness. No matter how terrible your sins, God loves you. If it were
not for the love of God, none of us would ever have a chance in
the future life. But God is love! And His love for us is everlasting."[1]

This is what Annie discovered. It seems that she felt unlovable
because of a deep trauma she'd experienced as a child. To make
matters worse, she'd contracted a devastating disease, making her
feel that God had rejected her.

Terri, her husband, Dave, and I began to pray God's love and
healing over Annie. As we prayed, I felt the Holy Spirit's presence.
That's when Terri began to pray against the shame Annie felt as

a child. When Terri finished praying, I opened my eyes and got a shock. My friend's face actually glowed.

"Annie, you look so different!" I exclaimed.

"I feel different!" she said.

"Your eyes! There's such a peace," I said.

Terri said, "It's like a light is shining."

Annie explained, "I feel God's love shining on me."

Annie will never be the same after such a loving encounter with the Lord.[2]

God loves Annie, and he loves you just as much. How much would your life change if you could grasp God's love for you? For one thing, when you begin to comprehend God's love for you, then you can learn how to love your neighbor as yourself. You will be able to love your neighbor as the love of God pours through you. Trying to love your neighbor without the power of God's love activated in you is hollow. You must learn how to receive God's love for yourself before you can love others through God's love.

Author James Bryan Smith said, "God's love comes down to us, fills our hearts, and is then extended to our neighbor. When we know and feel and experience God's love we cannot *but* love ourselves. This kind of self-love is nothing like the cheap form of narcissism peddled in our culture. It is a genuine, comprehensive kind of love that is based not on what we do but on who we are."[3]

Name above All Names

One of God's key attributes is love. In fact, God *is* love. The apostle John described it like this:

> Dear friends, we must love each other because love comes from God. Everyone who loves has been born from God and knows God. The person who doesn't love doesn't know God, because God is

love. God has shown us his love by sending his only Son into the world so that we could have life through him. This is love: not that we have loved God, but that he loved us and sent his Son to be the payment for our sins. (1 John 4:7–10 GW)

Because God loves us, we can love him in return and love others. Let's explore the promise garden of love to discover promises concerning:

- God's love for us
- our love for God
- our love for others

THE PROMISE GARDEN OF LOVE

GOD'S LOVE FOR US

Your Word says: "Hope never makes us ashamed because the love of God has come into our hearts through the Holy Spirit Who was given to us" (Rom. 5:5 NLV).

I agree: I am never ashamed that my hope is in you, Lord, because you have gifted my heart with your love through the Holy Spirit. Thank you!

Your Word says: "No, despite all these things, overwhelming victory is ours through Christ, who loved us. And I am convinced that nothing can ever separate us from God's love. Neither death nor life, neither angels nor demons, neither our fears for today nor our worries about tomorrow—not even the powers of hell can separate us from God's love. No power in the sky above or in the earth below—indeed, nothing in all creation will ever be able to separate us from the love of God that is revealed in Christ Jesus our Lord" (Rom. 8:37–39 NLT).

I agree: No matter my circumstances, I have overwhelming victory through Christ Jesus, who loves me. Nothing, including death, life, angels, demons, fear, or worry, can separate me from your love, Lord. Your love holds fast even against the powers of hell, against any power in the heavens or in the depths of the earth. In fact, nothing in all of creation can separate me from your love, which you revealed to me in Christ Jesus my Lord.

Your Word says: "I love those who love me, and those who seek me diligently find me" (Prov. 8:17 ESV).

I agree: I have looked for you and found you, Lord. As my love for you grows, your love for me becomes my everything.

Your Word says: "See how very much our Father loves us, for he calls us his children, and that is what we are!" (1 John 3:1 NLT).

I agree: How much you love me! You call me your child, and I am!

Your Word says: "O Lord, you are so good, so ready to forgive, so full of unfailing love for all who ask for your help" (Ps. 86:5 NLT).

I agree: Lord, you are so good to me, always ready to forgive. Your unfailing love surrounds me when I ask you for help.

OUR LOVE FOR GOD

Your Word says: "But if anyone loves God, he is known by God" (1 Cor. 8:3 ESV).

I agree: I love you, Lord! This means you know me.

<hr />

Your Word says: "You are my friends if you obey my commandments. I don't call you servants anymore, because a servant doesn't know what his master is doing. But I've called you friends because I've made known to you everything that I've heard from my Father" (John 15:14–15 GW).

I agree: I am your friend, Jesus, because I obey your commandments. You don't call me your servant; you call me your friend and show me all that your Father reveals to you.

OUR LOVE FOR OTHERS

Your Word says: "Above all, love each other deeply, because love covers over a multitude of sins" (1 Pet. 4:8 NIV).

I agree: Above all, show me how to love others more deeply and not to focus on their flaws, irritating behaviors, or wrongs. Through you, my love for them will cover their failings.

<hr />

Your Word says: "I give you a new Law. You are to love each other. You must love each other as I have loved you. If you love each other, all men will know you are My followers" (John 13:34–35 NLV).

I agree: Lord, you have told me to love those you have put in my life in the same way you love me. When I love others, then everyone will know I belong to you.

—

Your Word says: "Love your enemies! Do good to them. Lend to them without expecting to be repaid. Then your reward from heaven will be very great, and you will truly be acting as children of the Most High, for he is kind to those who are unthankful and wicked" (Luke 6:35 NLT).

I agree: I understand that you want me to not only do good to my enemies but also love them. You want me to lend to them without expecting anything in return. Then my reward in heaven will be great, for I will be acting as your child. (Which I am!) You illustrate to me how to be kind to the ungrateful as well as the dreadful. Help me to follow your lead.

—

Dear Lord,

Thank you for these promises regarding your love. I say yes and agree with them and believe they are for me. Give me even more faith to believe as I cling to your Word. I pray this in the power of the name of Jesus. Yes and amen.

17

Peace

You will keep in perfect peace
all who trust in you,
all whose thoughts are fixed on you!
Isaiah 26:3 NLT

Max Lucado, in his book *Traveling Light*, said, "Anxiety is an expensive habit. Of course, it might be worth the cost if it worked. But it doesn't. Our frets are futile. Jesus said, 'You cannot add any time to your life by worrying about it' (Matt. 6:27). Worry has never brightened a day, solved a problem, or cured a disease."[1]

Why carry worries around if they don't help? I once tried to get this point across to a young woman who was carrying many deep-seated worries. She explained, "It's just that I feel that something terrible is about to happen, like a dark unnamed disaster is about to rise up and overwhelm me."

I argued, "But what if that's not the case? What if this is actually the dawn of a beautiful day in a wonderful season of your life? There you are in your little boat, enjoying the sunrise. But you stop looking up and try to peer into the dark waters beneath you. Could something be just beneath the surface ready to strike, to topple you?"

Her shoulders slumped. "Yes, that's what I mean. That's exactly how I feel."

"But what if the only way your boat could topple was if you were leaning over trying to fish for something that doesn't even exist?"

"I never thought of it like that."

My friend needed to stop poking around in her sea of worries. I told her, "You need to look up and look into God's smiling face. And even if something does happen, God will be there to help you through. If you ask him, he'll even help you put up a 'No Fishing' sign."

"What do you mean?" she asked.

"Stop fishing in your sea of worries. Stop worrying about your fears. Look to God and enjoy his peace and the beauty of this new day."

Author Ann Spangler explained peace in this way: "To experience peace in its fullness is to experience healing, satisfaction, prosperity. To be at peace is to be happy, fulfilled. It is a sign of the blessed life, of the new creation. Peace has a whiff of paradise about it. It offers us a taste of the world to come."[2]

So get out there and rest in God's peace and enjoy this beautiful day.

Name above All Names

One of God's names, *Adonai Shalom*, means "the Lord is peace."

We see this name of the Lord used in his encounter with Gideon, a young man who felt he was the least in his father's house and spent a lot of time trying to hide his crops from the enemies of his land. But the angel of the Lord appeared to Gideon while Gideon was in the winepress, trying to thresh his wheat.

The angel of the Lord told Gideon that he was a warrior and that it was up to him to stop the marauders who'd been plundering the land and stealing his people's livestock and crops. Gideon was so shocked by this message that he asked for proof that the visitor was indeed from the Lord. The proof came in an unusual way. When Gideon brought the angel an offering of seared goat, broth, and unleavened bread, the angel instructed Gideon to pour out the broth and to place the meat and the unleavened bread on a rock. When Gideon complied, the angel touched the rock with his staff, and a flame flared from the rock and the food disappeared. Then so did the angel. Gideon was so afraid that he was about to die that he cried out, "Alas, Sovereign LORD! I have seen the angel of the LORD face to face" (Judg. 6:22 NIV).

But the Lord said to Gideon, "Peace! Do not be afraid. You are not going to die" (v. 23 NIV). So Gideon built an altar there to *Adonai* and called it *Adonai Shalom*.

This name of God is also a word of encouragement to you. Peace to you. Fear not.

Perhaps you are like Gideon. You're trying to hide from your fears when what you really need to do is draw near to God and discover his promises for you in your situation, then learn how to apply them. Author Nick Harrison said, "Sometimes it seems like God sees to it that we have plenty of opportunities to put his promises to use. Those opportunities usually go by names like trouble, worry, illness, financial loss, broken relationships and more. When we have such deep needs in our lives, when we listen closely, we can hear God calling, "Come closer, come closer."[3]

Let's move closer to God as we explore his promises concerning peace. We will also discover ways to find peace by:

- overcoming conflict
- overcoming fear
- overcoming worry

THE PROMISE GARDEN OF PEACE

Your Word says: "Then you will experience God's peace, which exceeds anything we can understand. His peace will guard your hearts and minds as you live in Christ Jesus" (Phil. 4:7 NLT).

I agree: Lord, I may not be able to understand it, but I know that your peace guards my heart and mind as I live in Christ Jesus.

Your Word says: "You will keep in perfect peace all who trust in you, all whose thoughts are fixed on you!" (Isa. 26:3 NLT).

I agree: When I trust in and focus my thoughts on you, Lord, you will keep me in perfect peace.

Your Word says: "I am leaving you with a gift—peace of mind and heart. And the peace I give is a gift the world cannot give. So don't be troubled or afraid" (John 14:27 NLT).

I agree: Your gift of peace of mind and heart is unlike anything the world can give me. Therefore, I have no reason to be troubled or afraid.

Your Word says: "Therefore, since we have been made right in God's sight by faith, we have peace with God because of what Jesus Christ our Lord has done for us" (Rom. 5:1 NLT).

I agree: You see me as righteous because of my faith in you. I have your peace because of what Jesus Christ did for me.

Your Word says: "I have said these things to you, that in me you may have peace. In the world you will have tribulation. But take heart; I have overcome the world" (John 16:33 ESV).

I agree: Lord, thank you for sharing your promises with me so that I can have peace. Even though this world will trouble me with trials and tribulations, I will take heart because you have overcome the world.

OVERCOMING CONFLICT

Your Word says: "Those who promote peace have joy" (Prov. 12:20 NIV).

I agree: I will promote your peace and happily receive your joy.

Your Word says: "Blessed are those who make peace. They will be called God's children" (Matt. 5:9 GW).

I agree: I am blessed because I am a peacemaker. That's why people know I belong to you.

Your Word says: "If your brother sins against you, go and tell him what he did without other people hearing it. If he listens to you, you have won your brother back again" (Matt. 18:15 NLV).

I agree: If someone sins against me, I will discuss it with them in private. If they listen, I will win them back.

Your Word says: "Those who guard their mouths and their tongues keep themselves from calamity" (Prov. 21:23 NIV).

I agree: Just by putting a guard on my words, I will prevent problems.

Your Word says: "A hot-tempered person stirs up conflict, but the one who is patient calms a quarrel" (Prov. 15:18 NIV).

I agree: Losing my temper only creates more conflict. If I am patient in a quarrel, I will help bring peace.

OVERCOMING FEAR

Your Word says: "For God has not given us a spirit of fear and timidity, but of power, love, and self-discipline" (2 Tim. 1:7 NLT).

I agree: Lord, you do not give me fear or cause me to be timid. You give me power, love, and self-control.

Your Word says: "There is no fear in love. Perfect love puts fear out of our hearts" (1 John 4:18 NLV).

I agree: There is no fear in love because love cancels fear.

Your Word says: "This is my command—be strong and courageous! Do not be afraid or discouraged. For the LORD your God is with you wherever you go" (Josh. 1:9 NLT).

I agree: You command me to be strong and courageous. I do not need to be afraid or discouraged, for you, Lord, are with me everywhere I go.

Your Word says: "Even when I walk through the darkest valley, I will not be afraid, for you are close beside me. Your rod and your staff protect and comfort me" (Ps. 23:4 NLT).

I agree: Lord, I am not afraid, even in the darkest valleys, with you by my side. I know you are equipped to protect me with your comfort and care.

Your Word says: "I, the LORD your God, hold your right hand and say to you, 'Don't be afraid; I will help you'" (Isa. 41:13 GW).

I agree: You hold my right hand and tell me that you will help me. I do not need to be afraid.

Your Word says: "A person's fear sets a trap for him, but one who trusts the LORD is safe" (Prov. 29:25 GW).

I agree: Fear is a trap. That is why I choose to trust you, Lord.

OVERCOMING WORRY

Your Word says: "Give all your worries and cares to God, for he cares about you" (1 Pet. 5:7 NLT).

I agree: Lord, I present you with all my cares and worries. You don't want me to carry them because you care about me.

Your Word says: "Do not worry. Learn to pray about everything. Give thanks to God as you ask Him for what you need. The peace of God is much greater than the human mind can understand. This peace will keep your hearts and minds through Christ Jesus" (Phil. 4:6–7 NLV).

I agree: I am not worried because I talk to you about everything. I thank you for your provision as I tell you what I need. Your peace is greater than what I can understand. Your peace keeps my heart and mind focused on you.

Your Word says: "When my worry is great within me, your comfort brings joy to my soul" (Ps. 94:19 NLV).

I agree: When worries rise within me, you comfort me so that joy fills my soul.

⟊

Your Word says: "And we know that God causes everything to work together for the good of those who love God and are called according to his purpose for them" (Rom. 8:28 NLT).

I agree: You, Lord, work everything for my good and for the purpose you have in mind for me. Somehow, you use even my mistakes and circumstances and turn them into good. You do this because you are working miracles into my life.

⟊

Dear Lord,

Thank you for these promises regarding peace. I say yes and agree with them and believe they are for me. Give me even more faith to believe as I cling to your Word. I pray this in the power of the name of Jesus. Yes and amen.

18

Presence of God

And remember that I am always with you until the
end of time.

Matthew 28:20 GW

Cynthia grew up in a Christian home and came to faith as a child,
but as she grew older, she began to ask questions such as, "How
likely is it that I was born into the correct religion? How strong is
the evidence for the God of the Bible?"

Not only was she not able to find the answers to her questions,
but she also wasn't impressed with some of the Christians she
knew. Soon Cynthia began to construct her own philosophy of
life apart from God.

After high school, she was thrilled to enter a secular school
where she studied nursing. The courses were hard, and many students dropped out. Cynthia said, "We attended a human anatomy
class at a nearby university. Older nursing students would reassure
us that we could take the class again in the summer if we earned

poor grades. Needless to say, many freshman nurses reacted with terror to our first anatomy test. The night before, I recall watching one frantic girl run around in the fallen leaves outside my dorm window. I couldn't help but think, *What a ridiculous thing to do*."

Still, Cynthia was nervous about the test, and when she sat down at her desk to study, she decided to pray for the first time in years. "God, if you are there, will you help me?"

She was surprised to hear his still, small voice assure her, *I have promised*.

She asked, "What do you mean you have promised?"

That's when her eyes landed on the Bible sitting by her nursing books, and she thought about all the promises she had all but forgotten.

I will never leave you or forsake you, popped into her thoughts, and she knew she had her answer.

Cynthia said, "I went on to score well on the test. That was the year I began to walk back to God. Much later, I found a young man who could give deep answers to many of my nagging questions."

Cynthia was glad that God brought her home to himself because, as she said, "I belonged to him."[1]

God's presence is always with us, even when we stray. But just because God's presence is with us doesn't mean we always walk in the Spirit. Henry Blackaby and Richard Blackaby, in *Discovering God's Daily Agenda*, said, "Walking in the Spirit is a choice we make. It involves choosing—moment by moment—to live under the direction and in the power of the Holy Spirit. Walking in the flesh will always produce sin. Walking in the Spirit will always result in righteousness. Life's situations are opportunities for the Spirit residing in Christians to live out His life through them and to reveal to a watching world what He is like."[2]

Name above All Names

One of God's names is *Jehovah Shammah*, which means "the Lord is my companion, his presence is with me." Jesus himself said, "And remember that I am always with you until the end of time" (Matt. 28:20 GW).

This is an incredible promise, because there was a time when God's presence rested on a box, namely, the ark of the covenant, a golden chest the Israelites carried on poles as they moved their tent tabernacle around in the desert.

But then Jesus came to dwell with us on earth, and when he returned to heaven, he sent us the Comforter, the Holy Spirit. When we follow Jesus, the Comforter comes to us, and we are transformed, becoming living, breathing "arks of the covenant." Instead of resting on a box in a tent, the presence of God rests in our hearts.

Let's find out more about the presence of God and the indwelling of the Holy Spirit by exploring the promise garden of the presence of God.

THE PROMISE GARDEN OF THE PRESENCE OF GOD

Your Word says: "The LORD replied, 'My Presence will go with you, and I will give you rest'" (Exod. 33:14 NIV).

I agree: I am so glad that your presence goes with me. Thank you for giving me rest.

Your Word says: "You will seek me and find me, when you seek me with all your heart" (Jer. 29:13 ESV).

I agree: I am seeking you with all my heart. Thank you that I can find you.

Your Word says: "No one has ever seen God. If we love each other, God lives in us, and his love is perfected in us" (1 John 4:12 GW).

I agree: I may not have seen you with my eyes, but I know that you live inside me. Your love is perfected in me as I learn how to give it to others.

Your Word says: "For where two or three are gathered in my name, there am I among them" (Matt. 18:20 ESV).

I agree: When I gather with two or three believers, your presence is with us.

Your Word says: "Be strong and courageous. Do not be afraid or terrified because of them, for the LORD your God goes with you; he will never leave you nor forsake you" (Deut. 31:6 NIV).

I agree: I am strong and courageous, and I am not afraid or terrified because of my enemy. Why should I be? You, Lord, go with me, and you will never leave or forsake me.

Your Word says: "We know how much God loves us, and we have put our trust in his love. God is love, and all who live in love live in God, and God lives in them" (1 John 4:16 NLT).

I agree: Because I know your deep love, Lord, I put my trust in you. You are love, and when I love, I live in you and you live in me.

—

Your Word says: "I am with you and will watch over you wherever you go, and I will bring you back to this land. I will not leave you until I have done what I have promised you" (Gen. 28:15 NIV).

I agree: You are with me and watch over me wherever I go. You will bring me back to where I belong, and you will not leave me until you have done all you promised me.

—

Your Word says: "The LORD is near to everyone who prays to him, to every faithful person who prays to him" (Ps. 145:18 GW).

I agree: You are near to me, especially when I pray.

—

Your Word says: "And I will ask the Father, and he will give you another Helper, to be with you forever" (John 14:16 ESV).

I agree: Thank you for sending me the Holy Spirit, who will be with me forever.

—

Your Word says: "I will put my Spirit in you. I will enable you to live by my laws, and you will obey my rules" (Ezek. 36:27 GW).

I agree: You put your Holy Spirit in me so that I can live by your laws and obey your rules.

***

Your Word says: "You go before me and follow me. You place your hand of blessing on my head. Such knowledge is too wonderful for me, too great for me to understand! I can never escape from your Spirit! I can never get away from your presence" (Ps. 139:5–7 NLT).

I agree: You go before and behind me. You place your hand on my head and bless me. This is too wonderful for me to comprehend. I can never escape your Holy Spirit or remove myself from your presence.

***

Your Word says: "And because we are his children, God has sent the Spirit of his Son into our hearts, prompting us to call out, 'Abba, Father'" (Gal. 4:6 NLT).

I agree: I am your child, and you sent the Spirit into my heart, prompting me to call you my dear Father.

***

Your Word says: "Christ gave you the Holy Spirit and He lives in you. You do not need anyone to teach you. The Holy Spirit is able to teach you all things. What He teaches you is truth and not a lie. Live by the help of Christ as the Holy Spirit has taught you" (1 John 2:27 NLV).

I agree: Jesus, you gave me the Holy Spirit, who lives in me. The Spirit is my teacher and shows me what is true and what is a lie. I live by your help and all that the Holy Spirit has taught me.

Dear Lord,

Thank you for these promises regarding your presence and the Holy Spirit. I say yes and agree with them and believe they are for me. Give me even more faith to believe as I cling to your Word. I pray this in the power of the name of Jesus. Yes and amen.

19

Protection

You, O LORD, are my refuge! You have made the Most
High your home. No harm will come to you. No sickness will come near your house. He will put his angels
in charge of you to protect you in all your ways.

Psalm 91:9–11 GW

Sheila Walsh told a story about the time she was camping in the
eastern highlands of Scotland when a storm hit. She weathered
the storm by hiding inside her sleeping bag in a nearby cave. The
wind howled, but Sheila was completely sheltered. She said, "No
matter what may be raging around you at this very moment, God's
promises offer shelter and cover when you feel most vulnerable
and alone."[1]

My friend Rhonda has seen the power of God's protection for
her children. Recently, I got an email from Rhonda describing her
daughter's misadventure on a Missouri freeway. Rhonda wrote,
"My daughter was on 270 going 70 miles an hour. A semitruck

driver didn't see her and hit her from the rear. A semi! Seventy miles an hour on one of the busiest, craziest highways in St. Louis. She doesn't have a scratch. The car is a bit messed up, but she was still able to drive it. She went on to work. There was so clearly a God intervention there. I'm amazed and so very thankful."

Later, when Rhonda and I were talking by phone, I told her, "You know, people don't get hit by semitrucks going 70 miles an hour and walk away, much less drive away."

"I know," Rhonda said. "If you ever saw that part of 270, you would say her escape was miraculous."

"You've been praying Psalm 91 over your children, haven't you?" I asked.

"I'm not sure."

I could hear the pages of Rhonda's Bible rustling. Then she came back on the line. "Yes, I not only pray that passage over my kids every day, but I also sing it! I just didn't recognize the reference."[2]

Psalm 91 is one of the oldest psalms in the Bible and is loaded with powerful promises. I believe God honored his promises over Rhonda's daughter because Rhonda claimed them for her kids.

You'll find Psalm 91 in the promise garden of protection for you to pray over yourself and your loved ones.

Name above All Names

We know that our God is our protector, as Psalm 20:1 describes: "The LORD will answer you in times of trouble. The name of the God of Jacob will protect you" (GW). "The God of Jacob," *Elohe Yakob*, protects his people.

God certainly protected Jacob. Jacob's twin brother, Esau, sold Jacob his inheritance for a bowl of stew. Then when their old, blind father called for Esau so he could give him the firstborn blessing,

Jacob disguised himself as his brother and received the blessing for himself. After that, fearing for his life, Jacob ran away to escape his brother's wrath.

But God not only protected Jacob from the wrath of his brother but also blessed Jacob to become the father of the twelve tribes of Israel.

God also blesses us today with his promises of protection and justice, as we will see in the promise garden of protection.

The Promise Garden of Protection

Your Word says: "Whoever lives under the shelter of the Most High will remain in the shadow of the Almighty. I will say to the LORD, 'You are my refuge and my fortress, my God in whom I trust.' He is the one who will rescue you from hunters' traps and from deadly plagues. He will cover you with his feathers, and under his wings you will find refuge. His truth is your shield and armor. You do not need to fear terrors of the night, arrows that fly during the day, plagues that roam the dark, epidemics that strike at noon. They will not come near you, even though a thousand may fall dead beside you or ten thousand at your right side. You only have to look with your eyes to see the punishment of wicked people. You, O LORD, are my refuge! You have made the Most High your home. No harm will come to you. No sickness will come near your house. He will put his angels in charge of you to protect you in all your ways. They will carry you in their hands so that you never hit your foot against a rock. You will step on lions and cobras. You will trample young lions and snakes. Because you love me, I will rescue you. I will protect you because you know my name. When you call to me, I will answer you. I will be with you when you are in trouble. I will save you and honor you. I will satisfy you with a long life. I will show you how I will save you" (Ps. 91 GW).

I agree: Most High, I live beneath your shelter and will remain under your shadow. You are my refuge and fortress, the God I trust. You rescue me from every trap and deadly plague. You cover me with your wings and hide me in your feathers. Your truth is my shield and armor. I do not need to fear the terrors in the night or the arrows that fly during the day or the plagues or epidemics that hide in darkness or strike at noon. These calamities will not come near me, even if a thousand or ten thousand fall dead beside me. I can see your punishment of the wicked, but you are my refuge. You, Most High, are my home. No harm will come to me. No sickness will come near my house. You put your angels in charge over me to protect me in every way. Your angels will keep me from even stubbing my toe. I can step on and trample lions and cobras because you love me and rescue me. You protect me because I know your name. I call to you, and you answer me. You are with me in trouble. You save and honor me. You will satisfy me with a long life and will show me how you will save me.

––––

Your Word says: "God is our refuge and strength, a very present help in trouble" (Ps. 46:1 ESV).

I agree: Lord, you protect me. You are my refuge and strength, and you help me in times of trouble.

––––

Your Word says: "He will not let you stumble; the one who watches over you will not slumber. Indeed, he who watches over Israel never slumbers or sleeps. The LORD himself watches over you! The LORD stands beside you as your protective shade. The sun will not harm you by day, nor the moon at night. The LORD keeps you from all harm and watches over your life. The LORD keeps watch over you as you come and go, both now and forever" (Ps. 121:3–8 NLT).

I agree: Lord, I am grateful that you will never let me stumble. You never slumber, and you constantly watch over me. You stand beside me like protective shade. Neither the sun nor the moon can harm me. You keep me safe from harm as you watch over my life. You watch as I come and go, now and forever.

———

Your Word says: "But the Lord is faithful, and he will strengthen you and protect you from the evil one" (2 Thess. 3:3 NIV).

I agree: Lord, I am so blessed because you are faithful and you strengthen me as you protect me from the evil one.

———

Your Word says: "The LORD is on my side; I will not fear. What can man do to me" (Ps. 118:6 ESV).

I agree: You give me courage because you are at my side. I will not fear! I have you, Lord, so what can anyone do to me?

———

Your Word says: "Even when you are old I will be the same. And even when your hair turns white, I will help you. I will take care of what I have made. I will carry you, and will save you" (Isa. 46:4 NLV).

I agree: Lord, you never age! Even when I am old, you will be the same. Even when my hair turns white, you will continue to help me. You will take care of all my concerns. You will carry me and save me.

—

Your Word says: "The name of the LORD is a strong tower; the righteous man runs into it and is safe" (Prov. 18:10 ESV).

I agree: You are my strength! I run to you, my strong tower. You keep me safe.

—

Your Word says: "The LORD will fight for you; you need only to be still" (Exod. 14:14 NIV).

I agree: You fight for me. I only need to be still. Let me rest in you and watch you win my battles.

—

Your Word says: "My God is my rock, in whom I find protection. He is my shield, the power that saves me, and my place of safety. He is my refuge, my savior, the one who saves me from violence. I called on the LORD, who is worthy of praise, and he saved me from my enemies" (2 Sam. 22:3–4 NLT).

I agree: I will hide myself in you because you are my rock, in whom I find protection. You are my shield, the power that saves me, and my place of safety. You are my refuge, my Savior, and the one who saves me from violence. I call on you, Lord. You are worthy of praise, and you save me from my enemies.

Your Word says: "I fall asleep in peace the moment I lie down because you alone, O LORD, enable me to live securely" (Ps. 4:8 GW).

I agree: When my head hits the pillow, I fall asleep in peace, because you and you alone cause me to be safe.

Your Word says: "You hide them in the secret place of your presence from those who scheme against them. You keep them in a shelter, safe from quarrelsome tongues" (Ps. 31:20 GW).

I agree: I am hidden in you. Your presence is my secret place from those who would scheme against me. You are my shelter, a safe place from quarreling, angry words.

Your Word says: "The LORD protects them and keeps them alive. He gives them prosperity in the land and rescues them from their enemies" (Ps. 41:2 NLT).

I agree: Lord, thank you for protecting me and keeping me alive. You give me prosperity in my land and rescue me from my enemies.

Your Word says: "We know the God who said, 'I alone have the right to take revenge. I will pay back.' God also said, 'The Lord will judge his people'" (Heb. 10:30 GW).

I agree: I will honor your request and listen as you tell me I should not take revenge on my enemies. Revenge is saved for you and you alone, Lord. You will judge your people.

Your Word says: "Turn from evil and do good, and you will live in the land forever. For the Lord loves justice, and he will never abandon the godly" (Ps. 37:27–28 NLT).

I agree: I turn from evil to do good and will live in your land forever. You love justice and will never abandon me.

Your Word says: "Let true justice prevail, so you may live and occupy the land that the LORD your God is giving you" (Deut. 16:20 NLT).

I agree: Because your true justice will prevail, I can occupy the land that you are giving me.

Your Word says: "Blessed are those who defend justice and do what is right at all times" (Ps. 106:3 GW).

I agree: I am blessed because I defend justice and seek to do what is right at all times.

Your Word says: "When justice is done, it brings joy to the righteous but terror to evildoers" (Prov. 21:15 NIV).

I agree: Lord, your justice brings joy to the righteous and terror to those who do evil.

Your Word says: "He makes sure orphans and widows receive justice. He loves foreigners and gives them food and clothes" (Deut. 10:18 GW).

I agree: You love those who are marginalized. You make orphans and widows receive justice. You love foreigners and provide for them in every way.

―

Dear Lord,

Thank you for these promises regarding protection and justice. I say yes and agree with them and believe they are for me. Give me even more faith to believe as I cling to your Word. I pray this in the power of the name of Jesus. Yes and amen.

20

Provision

Seek the Kingdom of God above all else, and live righteously, and he will give you everything you need.

Matthew 6:33 NLT

Sheila Walsh said, "How sad it would be to never have the privilege of going to our heavenly Father to meet our needs. He has every provision we need. He loves it when we ask, when we acknowledge our need for Him in our lives."[1]

My friend Karen Whiting has often experienced God's provision, especially at the dinner hour. She told me that when her husband retired from the Coast Guard, his anticipated job dried up. "We needed to live on two-thirds less income and still feed our five children."

To complicate matters, their three teens often brought friends home for dinner. Because their friends faced TV dinners at home alone, Karen and her husband didn't have the heart to turn them away. Karen said, "We trusted God to provide enough food for a dozen or more mouths every night, and he always did, for sixteen months straight."

Karen generally tossed flour, water, and yeast in a bread machine to prepare dough for pretzels to add bulk to the meals. She enlisted the visiting teens into rolling, shaping, and topping the pretzels with cheese, oil, and salt. "Helping to cook made the kids feel welcomed and part of our family," Karen said. "Every night as I put away the dishes, I always thanked God for his provision."[2]

God met Karen's needs so that she could meet the needs of those hungry teenagers.

Sheila Walsh said, "God is faithful, and His provision will be in keeping with the wealth of His mercy demonstrated in Jesus Christ."[3]

Name above All Names

It's really not surprising that one of God's names is *Jehovah Jireh*, meaning "the Lord will provide."

This name was revealed when Abraham was ordered to take his precious son, the child God had promised him in his old age, to be sacrificed on an altar.

Upon hearing this command, Abraham bundled the wood, prepared live coals for the fire, and took his own dear son to the place God had indicated. As the boy Isaac carried the firewood, he asked his father, "Where's the sacrificial lamb?"

"God will provide," the old man answered.

But it wasn't until Abraham's knife was poised over Isaac that the Lord told Abraham to stop.

In the end, God provided a ram for Abraham's sacrifice in place of Isaac.

Isn't this the same way that God provided his Son, who became our sacrificial lamb, as the sacrifice for our sins? Yes, God is still our provider.

As we tour the promise garden of provision, we will discover more of God's promises concerning how he provides for us and how we can use what he gives us to help others.

THE PROMISE GARDEN OF PROVISION

Your Word says: "And my God will meet all your needs according to the riches of his glory in Christ Jesus" (Phil. 4:19 NIV).

I agree: God, how thankful I am that you meet all my needs according to the glorious riches of Jesus Christ.

Your Word says: "The young lions suffer want and hunger; but those who seek the LORD lack no good thing" (Ps. 34:10 ESV).

I agree: Young lions may go hungry, but those who seek you, Lord, will be satisfied, lacking no good thing.

Your Word says: "I am the LORD your God, who brought you up out of Egypt. Open wide your mouth and I will fill it" (Ps. 81:10 NIV).

I agree: You are the Lord who brought your people out of Egypt. You are my provider, for when I open my mouth, you fill it.

Your Word says: "Seek the Kingdom of God above all else, and live righteously, and he will give you everything you need" (Matt. 6:33 NLT).

I agree: Thank you for giving me all I need because I live righteously and seek your kingdom above all else.

Your Word says: "And God is able to bless you abundantly, so that in all things at all times, having all that you need, you will abound in every good work" (2 Cor. 9:8 NIV).

I agree: You bless me abundantly so that on all occasions and at all times, I have all I need. You even cause me to abound in my good works.

Your Word says: "Let them give thanks to the Lord for His loving-kindness and His great works to the children of men! For He fills the thirsty soul. And He fills the hungry soul with good things" (Ps. 107:8–9 NLV).

I agree: Lord, I am so thankful for your loving-kindness and your great works to me and my family. You fill my thirsty and hungry soul with good things.

Your Word says: "There is one who is free in giving, and yet he grows richer. And there is one who keeps what he should give, but he ends up needing more. The man who gives much will have much, and he who helps others will be helped himself" (Prov. 11:24–25 NLV).

I agree: When I freely give, I grow richer. When I keep what I should give, I grow in lack. When I give much, I have much. When I help others, I myself am helped.

~

Your Word says: "Give, and it will be given to you. You will have more than enough. It can be pushed down and shaken together and it will still run over as it is given to you. The way you give to others is the way you will receive in return" (Luke 6:38 NLV).

I agree: When I give, Lord, you give to me and I have more than enough. My cup overflows when I give out of my abundance or even my lack. The way I give to others is the way you give to me.

~

Your Word says: "Blessed are those who are generous, because they feed the poor" (Prov. 22:9 NLT).

I agree: When I am generous to the poor, I am blessed.

~

Your Word says: "He who gives to the poor will never want, but many bad things will happen to the man who shuts his eyes to the poor" (Prov. 28:27 NLV).

I agree: When I give to the poor, I will never be in want. But bad things happen to those who see the poor and look the other way.

Your Word says: "'Bring one-tenth of your income into the store-house so that there may be food in my house. Test me in this way,' says the LORD of Armies. 'See if I won't open the windows of heaven for you and flood you with blessings'" (Mal. 3:10 GW).

I agree: I will bring one-tenth of my income as an offering to you, Lord. I will test you, and you will provide for me and also be my provision. You will open the windows of heaven and flood me with your blessings.

Your Word says: "The master was full of praise. 'Well done, my good and faithful servant. You have been faithful in handling this small amount, so now I will give you many more responsibilities. Let's celebrate together!'" (Matt. 25:21 NLT).

I agree: Lord, when I handle small matters faithfully, you are pleased and will increase my responsibilities.

Your Word says: "Honor the LORD with your wealth and with the firstfruits of all your produce; then your barns will be filled with plenty, and your vats will be bursting with wine" (Prov. 3:9–10 ESV).

I agree: It is my joy to honor you, Lord, with my wealth and ac-complishments. My life will burst with good things from you.

Dear Lord,

Thank you for these promises of provision. I say yes and agree with them and believe they are for me. Give me even more faith to believe as I cling to your Word. I pray this in the power of the name of Jesus. Yes and amen.

21

Purpose

And we know that for those who love God all things
work together for good, for those who are called according to his purpose.

Romans 8:28 ESV

In my book *Winning Your Daily Spiritual Battles*, I wrote, "God
writes his purposes for us in our hearts. Though we may not have
the whole picture at any given time, that's okay. . . . We are called
to follow God's direction for our lives as best we can. It's while
we are on the way that our callings become clear."[1]

This statement was certainly true for me. When I was younger,
I never dreamed that one of God's purposes for me was to write
books. After all, I'd spent two summers of my college years as
a summer missionary. I'd worked with kids, led vacation Bible
schools across the great state of Texas, and had a wonderful time
working as the summer youth director in tiny churches. Nope,
my goal was to graduate from seminary with a master's degree

in Christian education with an emphasis on youth and children. I was passionate about teaching young people about God.

And I was set. I had my bachelor's degree under my belt, an acceptance letter from a prominent seminary, and approval for my fall enrollment.

But then a letter from the seminary arrived telling me that I had been dismissed for marrying an engineering student instead of a pastoral student. At the same time, my church's new pastor decided that his buddy from seminary should have my job as the youth director at the church.

I was twenty-one years old and devastated. I wondered, *What terrible thing could I have possibly done that God would take his calling away from me?*

I soon landed a job as a technical writer in a high-tech company. The work was boring, and I so terribly missed my dream of working for God.

I wish I'd better understood that I could trust God to work everything out for my good, because that's exactly what he was doing all along. It was no accident that I'd become a writer in the aftermath of losing my dream of seminary, because one day without warning, God whispered to my heart, *I want you to write books for me.* I was shocked, and shocked again when I received a couple contracts to write teen devotionals. Once they were published, I realized that even if I'd worked as a youth director for forty years straight, I probably would not have reached as many young people as I did with my teen devotionals, *Ryan's Trials* and *Kara's Quest*.

God hadn't taken his calling away from me. And even though my plans fell apart, *his* plans were going according to his purposes.

You too can trust God to lead you to your purpose. "All you have to do to find your purpose is to be willing to walk with him, then take your next step as soon as it presents itself."[2]

Name above All Names

One of God's names is *Jehovah Mekoddishkem*, which means "the Lord who sanctifies you and makes you holy." God is a God who has a plan for our lives and who sets us apart. And that is why he calls us to be holy and to obey his laws (Lev. 20:7–8). Peter explained in 1 Peter 1:15–16, "But just as he who called you is holy, so be holy in all you do; for it is written: 'Be holy, because I am holy'" (NIV).

As we become a holy people of purpose, people who are set apart from the world, we can rest in God, listen for his voice, and follow his leading so that we can step into all he has established for us to do. The prophet Jeremiah explained, "For I know the plans I have for you, declares the LORD, plans for welfare and not for evil, to give you a future and a hope" (Jer. 29:11 ESV).

As we explore the promise garden of purpose, we will also discover promises concerning:

- ministry/mission
- obedience
- priorities
- the will of God

THE PROMISE GARDEN OF PURPOSE

Your Word says: "But for this purpose I have raised you up, to show you my power, so that my name may be proclaimed in all the earth" (Exod. 9:16 ESV).

I agree: You have raised me up for a purpose, to show me your power so that your name may be proclaimed in all the earth. Help me to do all that you have in your heart for me to do.

━━

Your Word says: "For I know the plans I have for you, declares the LORD, plans for welfare and not for evil, to give you a future and a hope" (Jer. 29:11 ESV).

I agree: It is a relief to know that you have wonderful plans for me. You have plans for good and not for evil, plans to give me a future and a hope.

━━

Your Word says: "And we know that for those who love God all things work together for good, for those who are called according to his purpose" (Rom. 8:28 ESV).

I agree: Because I love you, Lord, all things work together for good, for I am called according to your purpose.

━━

Your Word says: "You did not choose me, but I chose you and appointed you so that you might go and bear fruit—fruit that will last—and so that whatever you ask in my name the Father will give you" (John 15:16 NIV).

I agree: I did not choose you. You chose me and appointed me to go and complete missions for your kingdom. Because you have called me, I know that whatever I ask in the name of Jesus you will give me.

⁓

Your Word says: "And I am sure of this, that he who began a good work in you will bring it to completion at the day of Jesus Christ" (Phil. 1:6 ESV).

I agree: You are not done with me. You began a good work in me and will bring it to completion the moment I take my final breath.

⁓

Your Word says: "He who calls you is faithful; he will surely do it" (1 Thess. 5:24 ESV).

I agree: You are faithful! You called me and will help me fulfill my purpose.

MINISTRY/MISSION

Your Word says: "Go therefore and make disciples of all nations, baptizing them in the name of the Father and of the Son and of the Holy Spirit, teaching them to observe all that I have commanded you. And behold, I am with you always, to the end of the age" (Matt. 28:19–20 ESV).

I agree: Jesus, I am humbled that you have called me to tell others about you, to bring people to be baptized in the name of the Father and the Son and the Holy Spirit, and to teach them to observe what you've commanded. Jesus, I know you are with me always.

⁓

Your Word says: "For so the Lord has commanded us, saying, 'I have made you a light for the Gentiles, that you may bring salvation to the ends of the earth'" (Acts 13:47 ESV).

I agree: You commanded me to be a light to those who do not yet know you so that your salvation can spread throughout the earth. Teach me how to shine your light.

Your Word says: "But you will receive power when the Holy Spirit comes upon you. And you will be my witnesses, telling people about me everywhere—in Jerusalem, throughout Judea, in Samaria, and to the ends of the earth" (Acts 1:8 NLT).

I agree: I received power when the Holy Spirit came upon me. I will be your witness, Lord, telling people about you.

Your Word says: "Before I formed you in the womb I knew you, before you were born I set you apart; I appointed you as a prophet to the nations" (Jer. 1:5 NIV).

I agree: You knew me even before you formed me in my mother's womb. Even before I was born, you set me apart to tell others the good news about you.

OBEDIENCE

Your Word says: "But this command I gave them: 'Obey my voice, and I will be your God, and you shall be my people. And walk in all the way that I command you, that it may be well with you'" (Jer. 7:23 ESV).

I agree: Because I want things to go well for me, I will walk in the way you command me. I will obey your voice, and you will be my God, and I will belong to you.

⁓

Your Word says: "But if you are careful to obey him, following all my instructions, then I will be an enemy to your enemies, and I will oppose those who oppose you" (Exod. 23:22 NLT).

I agree: I will be careful to obey you and to follow all your instructions. In exchange, you promise that you will be an enemy to my enemies and will oppose those who oppose me.

⁓

Your Word says: "Jesus replied, 'Anyone who loves me will obey my teaching. My Father will love them, and we will come to them and make our home with them'" (John 14:23 NIV).

I agree: Jesus, you said that if I love you and obey your teachings, you will love me and make a home in me. You are welcome in my heart!

⁓

Your Word says: "He is working in you. God is helping you obey Him. God is doing what He wants done in you" (Phil. 2:13 NLV).

I agree: Lord, you are working in me, helping me to obey you. You are doing all that you want done in me.

⁓

Your Word says: "You are my friends if you do what I command" (John 15:14 NIV).

I agree: I love being your friend and will do what you command.

Your Word says: "He replied, 'Blessed rather are those who hear the word of God and obey it'" (Luke 11:28 NIV).

I agree: I am blessed when I hear your Word and obey it.

PRIORITIES

Your Word says: "Commit your work to the LORD, and your plans will be established" (Prov. 16:3 ESV).

I agree: I commit my work to you, Lord, and you will establish my plans.

Your Word says: "Whoever pursues righteousness and kindness will find life, righteousness, and honor" (Prov. 21:21 ESV).

I agree: What a promise. If I pursue righteousness and kindness, I will find life, righteousness, and honor.

Your Word says: "Whoever exalts himself will be humbled, and whoever humbles himself will be exalted" (Matt. 23:12 ESV).

I agree: I will not exalt myself so that you will not have to humble me. But when I am humble, you will exalt me.

Your Word says: "Whatever you do, work heartily, as for the Lord and not for men, knowing that from the Lord you will receive the inheritance as your reward. You are serving the Lord Christ" (Col. 3:23–24 ESV).

I agree: Whatever I am doing, I work heartily for you, Lord, and not for people. I know that I will receive joy through my salvation, for I am serving Jesus Christ.

THE WILL OF GOD

Your Word says: "The world and its desires pass away, but whoever does the will of God lives forever" (1 John 2:17 NIV).

I agree: The world and its desires will pass away, but the good news is that because I do your will, I will live forever.

Your Word says: "For whoever does the will of God, he is my brother and sister and mother" (Mark 3:35 ESV).

I agree: Lord, because I do your will, I am a member of your family.

Your Word says: "It is God's will that your honorable lives should silence those ignorant people who make foolish accusations against you" (1 Pet. 2:15 NLT).

I agree: It is your will that I live an honorable life. May my life silence any ignorant people who want to make foolish accusations against me.

Dear Lord,

Thank you for these promises regarding purpose, ministry/ mission, obedience, priorities, and the will of God. I say yes and agree with them and believe they are for me. Give me even more faith to believe as I cling to your Word. I pray this in the power of the name of Jesus. Yes and amen.

22

Relationships

Those who love other believers live in the light. Nothing will destroy the faith of those who live in the light.

1 John 2:10 GW

Wouldn't it be wonderful if every relationship could exist without conflict? I guess that day will come when we are all perfectly behaved on those heavenly streets of gold, but while we are here on earth, we need to walk through some messy situations. I like how my friend Janet Kobobel Grant explained God's take on our relationships: "He wants us to pray for resolutions of our differences in such a way that they bring glory to him rather than shame."[1]

No one has better illustrated this truth than my friend Dawn. Little did she know that her new husband had a secret: he was addicted to pornography. He covered his misbehavior with anger and accusations, leaving Dawn to feel hurt and as if she never measured up. Dawn begged Rick to get help for his anger, but he refused. After she found out about his addiction, he continued to distance himself from her, even using the men in his Bible study as a smoke screen. He had his friends all but convinced that Dawn was the real issue in their troubled marriage.

Dawn continued to lead the life of a faithful wife and good mother, devoting herself to her children, but inside she felt lonelier than ever. But her loneliness and grief became the catalyst that kept her on her knees. There she prayed that her husband would be set free from his addiction and that their marriage would be restored.

During this difficult time, Dawn found the inner strength she needed from Philippians 4:13: "I can do all things because Christ gives me the strength" (NLV). She also clung to Philippians 4:6–7: "Do not worry. Learn to pray about everything. Give thanks to God as you ask Him for what you need. The peace of God is much greater than the human mind can understand. This peace will keep your hearts and minds through Christ Jesus" (NLV).

One day Rick's Bible study friends told him they could no longer help him and that he needed to seek counsel from their pastor. During his sessions with the pastor, Rick began to deal with his own sexual abuse as a child. Two weeks later, Dawn found Rick in their kitchen sobbing. He pleaded, "Please forgive me for all I've put you through. I'm so sorry for all the years I've hurt you!"

The next day Rick called her with tears of joy. "During my prayer time today, I realized that God has forgiven me!"

That was the beginning of a new Rick—a Rick who was a new creature in Christ, a Rick who was set free from the power of pornography. His dramatic change happened over two years ago.

Dawn said, "It wasn't easy, but God restored our marriage. We now share a prayer and devotional time together, something that would never have happened before. He even helps others who are caught in the trap of porn addiction. It's amazing!"[2]

One lesson we can learn from Dawn's story is this: we don't have to convince God to love our loved ones. He already does. And his love for them is not based on their performance, attitudes, mistakes, or successes. In fact, God loves our loved ones even more than we do. Plus, God cares about our relationships with them. He will give us the strength to love them through his love, to forgive them through his power as he gifts us with more compassion, wisdom, and understanding.

It is also his will that every one of our loved ones should come to faith. He does not want even one of them to perish. So when you pray for their salvation, you are praying in his will, in agreement with him.

Name above All Names

We know that Jesus is God's Son and that God called Jesus the Redeemer through the prophet Isaiah: "The Redeemer will come to Zion, to those in Jacob who repent of their sins" (Isa. 59:20 NIV). The name *Redeemer* means "a person who redeems someone or something."[3]

Jesus redeemed, or restored, us to God. And as if that weren't enough, Jesus also redeemed or restored us to the people he has placed in our lives. This prayer by Max Lucado is most appropriate: "In my family, like most, we've had conflicts and unresolved issues. Help us today to put aside past hurts and to reconcile. Heal us, Lord, and restore our relationships."[4]

This kind of redemption and restoration is all about love, a love that first comes to us from God and then flows from us to others. As Jesus taught us in John 13:34, "I'm giving you a new commandment: Love each other in the same way that I have loved you" (GW).

Let's take a walk through the promise garden of relationships to discover the promises God has for us concerning:

- forgiving others
- friends
- husbands and wives
- parents and children
- singleness

THE PROMISE GARDEN OF RELATIONSHIPS

FORGIVING OTHERS

Your Word says: "For if you forgive other people when they sin against you, your heavenly Father will also forgive you. But if you do not forgive others their sins, your Father will not forgive your sins" (Matt. 6:14–15 NIV).

I agree: Lord, it's good when I forgive people who have wronged me. When I forgive others, you promise to forgive me. You won't forgive me when I don't forgive others. It's as simple as that.

Your Word says: "If you forgive the failures of others, your heavenly Father will also forgive you" (Matt. 6:14 GW).

I agree: Lord, you forgive me for my failures when I forgive others for theirs.

FRIENDS

Your Word says: "My command is this: Love each other as I have loved you. Greater love has no one than this: to lay down one's life for one's friends. You are my friends if you do what I command" (John 15:12–14 NIV).

I agree: Lord, you count me as a friend because I love others as you have loved me. There is no greater love than to spend my life serving my friends.

～

Your Word says: "Finally, all of you, be like-minded, be sympathetic, love one another, be compassionate and humble. Do not repay evil with evil or insult with insult. On the contrary, repay evil with blessing, because to this you were called so that you may inherit a blessing" (1 Pet. 3:8–9 NIV).

I agree: Lord, you help me build an inheritance of blessings when I share in your tenderheartedness, treating others humbly with love, sympathy, and compassion. I will not repay evil with evil or insult with insult. Instead, I will repay evil with blessings.

～

Your Word says: "Those who love other believers live in the light. Nothing will destroy the faith of those who live in the light" (1 John 2:10 GW).

I agree: When I walk in your love toward others, I walk in your light. This means that darkness will never destroy my faith.

～

Your Word says: "Walk with the wise and become wise; associate with fools and get in trouble" (Prov. 13:20 NLT).

I agree: When I walk with the wise, I become wise. This is why I will not join the company of fools or share in the trouble they create.

HUSBANDS AND WIVES

Your Word says: "Many waters cannot quench love; rivers cannot sweep it away" (Song of Sol. 8:7 NIV).

I agree: My wonderful Lord, the rough waters of life cannot sweep away my love for you or others.

Your Word says: "The man who finds a wife finds a treasure, and he receives favor from the LORD" (Prov. 18:22 NLT).

I agree: A wife is a blessing from the Lord and is both a treasure and a sign of the Lord's favor.

Your Word says: "Two are better than one, because they have a good reward for their toil" (Eccles. 4:9 ESV).

I agree: Two are better than one because they can accomplish more together.

Your Word says: "Your wife will be like a fruitful grapevine, flourishing within your home. Your children will be like vigorous young olive trees as they sit around your table" (Ps. 128:3 NLT).

I agree: A wife is like a gifted helpmate within my home. Children are like a garden of possiblities surrounding my table.

Your Word says: "In the same way, you husbands must give honor to your wives. Treat your wife with understanding as you live together. She may be weaker than you are, but she is your equal partner in God's gift of new life. Treat her as you should so your prayers will not be hindered" (1 Pet. 3:7 NLT).

I agree: Husbands should honor their wives and treat them with understanding. Wives may be weaker, but they are equal partners in God's gift of new life. A husband should treat his wife well so that his prayers will not be hindered.

PARENTS AND CHILDREN

Your Word says: "Children are a gift from the Lord; they are a reward from him. Children born to a young man are like arrows in a warrior's hands. How joyful is the man whose quiver is full of them! He will not be put to shame when he confronts his accusers at the city gates" (Ps. 127:3–5 NLT).

I agree: My children are a gift, a reward from you, Lord. They are like multiple arrows ready to shoot true. When my accusers see how excellent my children are, I will not be put to shame.

Your Word says: "He will turn the hearts of the parents to their children, and the hearts of the children to their parents" (Mal. 4:6 NIV).

I agree: I love that you will turn the hearts of parents to their children and the hearts of children to their parents.

—

Your Word says: "Discipline your children, and they will give you peace of mind and will make your heart glad" (Prov. 29:17 NLT).

I agree: I will discipline my children so that they will give me peace of mind and make my heart glad.

—

Your Word says: "The father of a righteous child has great joy; a man who fathers a wise son rejoices in him" (Prov. 23:24 NIV).

I agree: Righteous children bring their parents much joy. Wise children bring their parents much rejoicing.

SINGLENESS

Your Word says: "So you also are complete through your union with Christ, who is the head over every ruler and authority" (Col. 2:10 NLT).

I agree: In singleness, one is complete through their union with Christ, who is the head over every ruler and authority.

—

Your Word says: "So I say, walk by the Spirit, and you will not gratify the desires of the flesh" (Gal. 5:16 NIV).

I agree: I will walk by the Spirit and not give in to my earthly desires.

Your Word says: "No temptation has overtaken you that is not common to man. God is faithful, and he will not let you be tempted beyond your ability, but with the temptation he will also provide the way of escape, that you may be able to endure it" (1 Cor. 10:13 ESV).

I agree: No temptation can overtake me. God, you are faithful and will not let me be tempted beyond my ability but will provide a way of escape so that I can endure the temptation.

Your Word says: "Take delight in the LORD, and he will give you the desires of your heart" (Ps. 37:4 NIV).

I agree: I take delight in you, Lord, and you will give me the desires of my heart.

Dear Lord,

Thank you for these promises regarding forgiveness, friends, husbands and wives, parents and children, and singleness. I say yes and agree with them and believe you will fulfill them. Give me even more faith to believe as I cling to your Word. I pray this in the power of the name of Jesus. Yes and amen.

23

Salvation

For God so loved the world that he gave his one and
only Son, that whoever believes in him shall not perish
but have eternal life.

John 3:16 NIV

We are not holy enough to walk with a holy God because of our
sin. In Old Testament times, only the blood of sacrificed bulls and
goats could unite humans with God through a temporary bridge
of forgiveness, a bridge that would collapse as soon as a person
sinned again.

Jesus, God's own Son, came to this earth to become our permanent bridge to God.

Jesus, who never sinned, became our bridge to the Father by
becoming our sin and taking our punishment by dying on the
cross. Three days later, Jesus defeated sin and death by rising
from the dead. Because of his sacrifice for us, we can go to God

for forgiveness of sin and step out of Satan's kingdom of darkness into God's kingdom of light.

We can now approach God as though we were sinless. We can do this through the righteousness of our Lord and Savior, Jesus.

However, we must each, individually, agree to come under the blood covering of Jesus. Evangelist Billy Graham penned a prayer you can pray to help you receive forgiveness of sins and step into a right relationship with God:

> Dear Lord Jesus, I know that I am a sinner, and I ask for Your forgiveness. I believe You died for my sins and rose from the dead. I turn from my sins and invite You to come into my heart and life. I want to trust and follow You as my Lord and Savior. In Your Name. Amen.[1]

When you pray this kind of prayer for the first time, the Holy Spirit enters into your spirit. The Holy Spirit gives you power to live a new life in Christ and also breathes life into God's Word. You can always ask for more of the Holy Spirit, and he will give you more of his presence.

Those of us who follow Jesus long for our loved ones to also follow Jesus so that they will not suffer a hopeless eternity without the presence of God.

Author and friend Edie Melson told me, "I wanted more than anything for my daddy to spend eternity in heaven with me. But he was a proud intellectual, and the gospel was just too simple. Over the years, we had many conversations about God, salvation, and heaven. Some of them were good discussions; others were heated and hurtful—on both sides. Even his grandkids couldn't seem to reach him.

"I was about to give up when a promise in 1 Timothy leapt out at me. The promise read, 'Who [God our Savior] desires all men to be saved and to come to the knowledge of the truth'" (2:4 NASB).

Edie said, "It was almost as if God was urging me not to lose hope but to continue to pray for my father's salvation. I didn't see an immediate answer to my prayers, but I did feel a sense of peace that never left me as I continued to pray."

Several years later, Edie's father was diagnosed with vascular dementia and Alzheimer's disease. This revelation softened his heart in ways she never imagined, and thirty-three years from the first time she began praying for his salvation, her dad accepted the salvation Jesus offers.

Edie said, "It was a beautiful thing to see. I actually got to present the gospel and pray with him. There was a celebration throughout my entire church family because we'd been praying for him for so long. Daddy is gone now, but I know I will spend eternity with him. God is so amazing!"[2]

Name above All Names

The prophet Jeremiah prophesied about Jesus over six hundred years before Jesus was born to Mary, a virgin of King David's lineage. Jeremiah said:

> "For the time is coming," says the LORD, "when I will raise up a righteous descendant from King David's line. He will be a King who rules with wisdom. He will do what is just and right throughout the land. And this will be his name: 'The LORD Is Our Righteousness.'" (Jer. 23:5–6 NLT)

Jehovah Tsidkenu, "the Lord is our righteousness," is another name for God. It signifies that Jesus provides us with a robe of righteousness to wear before the Father.

Jesus once told a parable about this very thing. In this story, Jesus described a father planning a wedding for his son, but the guests on the original list refused to come, so the father sent his servants to the roadways, where they invited everyone to the feast.

Jesus said, "The servants went into the streets and brought in all the good people and all the evil people they found. And the wedding hall was filled with guests.

"When the king came to see the guests, he saw a person who was not dressed in the wedding clothes provided for the guests. He said to him, 'Friend, how did you get in here without proper wedding clothes?'

"The man had nothing to say. Then the king told his servants, 'Tie his hands and feet, and throw him outside into the darkness. People will cry and be in extreme pain there'" (Matt. 22:10–13 GW).

The meaning of Jesus's parable is clear: we may not enter into a relationship with God or into his eternal presence without the proper covering he has provided, namely, the righteousness of Jesus Christ.

When we stand before the Father, we do not do so in our own filthy rags, which represent our sin or our own feeble attempts to be made right with him. Instead, we are clothed in the salvation he has provided, the righteousness of Jesus, which covers our sins.

Let's visit the promise garden of salvation to see what other promises God provides for us regarding:

- forgiveness/redemption
- freedom
- grace
- Jesus Christ
- life in Christ
- overcoming sin

THE PROMISE GARDEN OF SALVATION

FORGIVENESS/REDEMPTION

Your Word says: "In him we have redemption through his blood, the forgiveness of sins, in accordance with the riches of God's grace" (Eph. 1:7 NIV).

I agree: Through you, Jesus, my sins have been redeemed. Through your blood, I have the forgiveness of sins through the richness of God's grace.

Your Word says: "Now repent of your sins and turn to God, so that your sins may be wiped away" (Acts 3:19 NLT)

I agree: I will not hesitate. I repent of my sins and turn to you. Praise God! My sins are wiped away.

Your Word says: "If we tell Him our sins, He is faithful and we can depend on Him to forgive us of our sins. He will make our lives clean from all sin" (1 John 1:9 NLV).

I agree: I confess my sins to you, Lord. You are faithful, and I know I can depend on you to forgive my sins. Through you, my life is counted clean of all sins.

Your Word says: "He has removed our sins as far from us as the east is from the west" (Ps. 103:12 NLT).

I agree: Lord, you have removed my sins from me as far as the east is from the west. What a relief.

Your Word says: "So now there is no condemnation for those who belong to Christ Jesus. And because you belong to him, the power of the life-giving Spirit has freed you from the power of sin that leads to death" (Rom. 8:1–2 NLT).

I agree: There is no condemnation for my sins because I belong to you, Jesus Christ. You have given me life through the Spirit and freed me from the power of sin that leads to eternal separation from you.

Your Word says: "For he has rescued us from the dominion of darkness and brought us into the kingdom of the Son he loves, in whom we have redemption, the forgiveness of sins" (Col. 1:13–14 NIV).

I agree: Lord, I have been rescued from the kingdom of darkness and brought into the kingdom of your beloved Son. Thank you that in Jesus I have redemption, the forgiveness of all my sins.

FREEDOM

Your Word says: "Then you will know the truth, and the truth will set you free" (John 8:32 NIV).

I agree: I know the truth. Jesus died for me! The truth has set me free.

~

Your Word says: "Out of my distress I called on the LORD; the LORD answered me and set me free" (Ps. 118:5 ESV).

I agree: When I was deep in my distress, I called to you, Lord, and you answered me and set me free.

~

Your Word says: "So if the Son sets you free, you will be free indeed" (John 8:36 ESV).

I agree: Jesus set me free from sin, and therefore, I am indeed free.

~

Your Word says: "Now the Lord is the Spirit, and where the Spirit of the Lord is, there is freedom" (2 Cor. 3:17 NIV).

I agree: You, Lord, are the Spirit, and wherever the Spirit of God is, there is freedom.

~

Your Word says: "For freedom Christ has set us free; stand firm therefore, and do not submit again to a yoke of slavery" (Gal. 5:1 ESV).

I agree: Jesus, you have set me free. I will stand firm and will not become a slave to sin again.

GRACE

Your Word says: "It is by grace you have been saved" (Eph. 2:5 NIV).

I agree: Yes! By the grace of God, I have been saved.

—

Your Word says: "Yet God, in his grace, freely makes us right in his sight. He did this through Christ Jesus when he freed us from the penalty for our sins" (Rom. 3:24 NLT).

I agree: Because of your unmerited kindness, God, you made me blameless in your sight. You did this through Jesus Christ and freed me from the penalty of my sins.

—

Your Word says: "For from his fullness we have all received, grace upon grace" (John 1:16 ESV).

I agree: Because God is without limitations, I have received his amazing grace in endless supply.

—

Your Word says: "But grace was given to each one of us according to the measure of Christ's gift" (Eph. 4:7 ESV).

I agree: I have been blessed with the lavish gift of Christ's grace.

—

Your Word says: "But he gives more grace. Therefore it says, 'God opposes the proud but gives grace to the humble'" (James 4:6 ESV).

I agree: God's grace is poured on the humble but kept from the proud.

—

Your Word says: "Let us then with confidence draw near to the throne of grace, that we may receive mercy and find grace to help in time of need" (Heb. 4:16 ESV).

I agree: Because of the grace of Jesus, I am not afraid to draw nearer to God. When I do, I find mercy and grace and all that I need.

—

Your Word says: "But he said to me, 'My grace is sufficient for you, for my power is made perfect in weakness.' Therefore I will boast all the more gladly of my weaknesses, so that the power of Christ may rest upon me" (2 Cor. 12:9 ESV).

I agree: Jesus said that his grace was enough for me. In fact, it is by his power that I am made perfect in weakness. Therefore, like the apostle Paul, I will gladly boast of my weaknesses so that the power of Christ can rest on me.

JESUS CHRIST

Your Word says: "For God so loved the world that he gave his one and only Son, that whoever believes in him shall not perish but have eternal life" (John 3:16 NIV).

I agree: God, you loved me and the people of the world so much that you sent your only Son Jesus so that anyone who believes in him will not die in their sins but will live with you forever.

Your Word says: "God made him who had no sin to be sin for us, so that in him we might become the righteousness of God" (2 Cor. 5:21 NIV).

I agree: God, you sent Jesus, who was sinless, to become my sin. It was the only way I could become righteous before you.

Your Word says: "For this is my blood, which confirms the covenant between God and his people. It is poured out as a sacrifice to forgive the sins of many" (Matt. 26:28 NLT).

I agree: The blood of Jesus seals the new covenant between God and his people. Jesus poured out his blood as a sacrifice so that he could forgive me of my sins.

Your Word says: "Christ carried our sins in his body on the cross so that freed from our sins, we could live a life that has God's approval. His wounds have healed you" (1 Pet. 2:24 GW).

I agree: My sins were in Christ's body on the cross. Because of this, I am free from my sins and can now obtain God's approval. The wounds of Jesus healed me and restored me to God.

Your Word says: "If you openly declare that Jesus is Lord and believe in your heart that God raised him from the dead, you will be saved" (Rom. 10:9 NLT).

I agree: I confess aloud that Jesus is Lord and believe in my heart that God raised him from the dead. I am saved!

Your Word says: "He is the one who forgives all your sins, the one who heals all your diseases" (Ps. 103:3 GW).

I agree: Praise God! Jesus forgives my sins and heals my diseases.

Your Word says: "Jesus spoke to the people once more and said, 'I am the light of the world. If you follow me, you won't have to walk in darkness, because you will have the light that leads to life'" (John 8:12 NLT).

I agree: Jesus is the light of the world. I follow him so that I am no longer in darkness. Through Jesus, I have the light that leads to life.

LIFE IN CHRIST

Your Word says: "Therefore, if anyone is in Christ, the new creation has come: The old has gone, the new is here!" (2 Cor. 5:17 NIV).

I agree: It's true. I am a new creation in Christ. The old is gone, replaced by the new!

Your Word says: "I will give them an undivided heart and put a new spirit in them; I will remove from them their heart of stone and give them a heart of flesh" (Ezek. 11:19 NIV).

I agree: My heart will no longer be divided because you, Lord, put a new spirit in me. You replaced my heart of stone with a heart of flesh.

***

Your Word says: "For we died and were buried with Christ by baptism. And just as Christ was raised from the dead by the glorious power of the Father, now we also may live new lives" (Rom. 6:4 NLT).

I agree: I died and was buried with Christ in baptism. Christ was raised from the dead by the power of the Father so that I might live a new life in Christ.

***

Your Word says: "But whoever drinks of the water that I will give him will never be thirsty again. The water that I will give him will become in him a spring of water welling up to eternal life" (John 4:14 ESV).

I agree: Jesus, when I drink your living water, my thirst is quenched and I know I will live forever with you.

***

Your Word says: "I have come into the world as light, so that whoever believes in me may not remain in darkness" (John 12:46 ESV).

I agree: I cannot remain in the dark because I have the light of Jesus.

Your Word says: "The thief comes only to steal and kill and destroy. I came that they may have life and have it abundantly" (John 10:10 ESV).

I agree: The devil wants to steal, kill, and destroy me, but Jesus came so that I may have abundant life.

OVERCOMING SIN

Your Word says: "Sin is no longer your master, for you no longer live under the requirements of the law. Instead, you live under the freedom of God's grace" (Rom. 6:14 NLT).

I agree: I am free because sin is no longer my master. I no longer live under the requirements of the law but in the freedom of God's grace.

Your Word says: "But you belong to God, my dear children. You have already won a victory over those people, because the Spirit who lives in you is greater than the spirit who lives in the world" (1 John 4:4 NLT).

I agree: I am God's dear child and belong to him. I have won a victory because the Holy Spirit lives in me and is greater than the spirit of the world.

Your Word says: "Submit yourselves therefore to God. Resist the devil, and he will flee from you" (James 4:7 ESV).

I agree: I give myself to you, God. I resist the devil, and he flees from me.

———

Dear Lord,

Thank you for these promises regarding forgiveness/redemption, freedom, grace, Jesus Christ, life in Christ, and overcoming sin. I say yes and agree with them and believe they are for me. Give me even more faith to believe as I cling to your Word. I pray this in the power of the name of Jesus. Yes and amen.

24

Strength

But those who trust in the LORD will find new
    strength.
    They will soar high on wings like eagles.
    They will run and not grow weary.
    They will walk and not faint.

                                        Isaiah 40:31 NLT

I know what it's like when human strength fails. When I was a
young married woman, my husband and I took off on our ten-
speed bicycles in 110-degree Texas heat to ride to a nearby town
for lunch.

The problem was the closer I got to the town, the slower I
pedaled. My husband rode up the next hill and missed that my
cycling speed had declined to the point that I could barely keep
my bike balanced. I eyed a shady spot on the side of the road and
wondered, *What if I were to lie down and just go to sleep?*

I knew this was a bad idea, but in the heat, I was no longer able to move forward. "Dear Lord, help me," I prayed as I dropped my bike and staggered toward the shade.

Just then Paul returned. He was alarmed when he saw me. "What are you doing?"

My words were sluggish. "I'm going to take a nap."

Paul's voice commanded, "Get back on your bike, and I'll push you."

So with one hand on the back of my bike seat, my strong young husband pedaled his bike up and down the Texas hills while pushing my bike beside his.

Finally, we made it to the cool of the restaurant, where we gulped gallons of iced tea. A couple hours later, with the temperature a dozen degrees lower, I was able to ride home under my own power.

What my husband did for me the day I lost my strength is the same thing that God will do for you when you lose your strength. Perhaps he'll power you down the paths you need to take or refresh you with his living water. All I know is that when you ask him for strength, he'll show up strong on your behalf.

Charles Stanley said:

> You and I are more likely to succeed in lifting a big rig truck with one finger than we are in handling the supernatural trials that assail us. Remember, "Our struggle is not against flesh and blood, but against the rulers, against the powers, against the world forces of the darkness, against the spiritual forces of wickedness in the heavenly places" (Eph. 6:12). If we insist on fighting these battles with our own strength, we will wear ourselves out and make no progress. But when you rely on God—when He is your energy and might—He empowers you, giving you resources that vastly surpass your human capabilities and that defy explanation.[1]

Name above All Names

One of God's names is *Elohei Ma'uzzi*, which means "God of my strength" or "strong fortress." We can find the warrior David using this name in 2 Samuel 22:33 after winning yet another battle with Saul. David sang, "God is my strong fortress; and He sets the blameless in His way" (NASB).

David was not the only biblical great who derived strength from God. So did Samson, one of the strongest men in the Bible. It took Samson a while to learn that his strength was not natural but supernatural. He revealed to his Philistine wife, Delilah, that the secret of his strength was in his hair. Later that same night, as Samson slept, the Philistines shaved his head.

The next day, with his strength gone, Samson was captured and blinded by the Philistines and thrown into prison. Some time later, the Philistines made the mistake of dragging Samson out of his cell so they could gloat over him while they feasted before their god Dagon. They placed him between two pillars. So tethered, Samson prayed to the Lord that his supernatural strength would return one last time. Then, with one mighty thrust, Samson knocked the pillars down, destroying the building and killing thousands of his enemy as well as himself.

This tragic story reveals that Samson, even as a ridiculed, blind captive held in chains, could use God's strength to eliminate many of Israel's enemies.

If Samson could use God's strength to do the impossible, think about what you could do if you called upon the strength of the Lord.

The promise garden of strength also contains promises regarding:

- courage
- overcoming weariness
- stability

THE PROMISE GARDEN OF STRENGTH

Your Word says: "He gives power to the weak and strength to the powerless" (Isa. 40:29 NLT).

I agree: Lord, help me whenever I am weak and powerless. I know you will give me your power and strength!

Your Word says: "But he said to me, 'My grace is sufficient for you, for my power is made perfect in weakness.' Therefore I will boast all the more gladly about my weaknesses, so that Christ's power may rest on me" (2 Cor. 12:9 NIV).

I agree: Your grace is sufficient for me, Lord. Your strength is made perfect in my weakness because Christ's power rests on me.

Your Word says: "Don't be afraid, for I am with you. Don't be discouraged, for I am your God. I will strengthen you and help you. I will hold you up with my victorious right hand" (Isa. 41:10 NLT).

I agree: I will not fear because you are with me. I will not be discouraged because you are my God. You strengthen and help me. You hold me up with your victorious right hand.

Your Word says: "But those who trust in the LORD will find new strength. They will soar high on wings like eagles. They will run and not grow weary. They will walk and not faint" (Isa. 40:31 NLT).

I agree: I trust in you, Lord. You help me find new strength. I will soar high on wings like eagles and will run and not grow weary. I will walk and not faint.

—

Your Word says: "For I can do everything through Christ, who gives me strength" (Phil. 4:13 NLT).

I agree: I can do everything you lead me to do through Christ's amazing strength.

—

Your Word says: "My flesh and my heart may fail, but God is the strength of my heart and my portion forever" (Ps. 73:26 ESV).

I agree: I know that my flesh and heart are weak and may fail. But God strengthens the heart of my soul so that I may live with him forever.

COURAGE

Your Word says: "So be strong and courageous! Do not be afraid and do not panic before them. For the LORD your God will personally go ahead of you. He will neither fail you nor abandon you" (Deut. 31:6 NLT).

I agree: I will be strong and courageous. There is no need to fear or panic, for you, Lord, go ahead of me. You will not fail or abandon me.

—

Your Word says: "This is my command—be strong and courageous! Do not be afraid or discouraged. For the LORD your God is with you wherever you go" (Josh. 1:9 NLT).

I agree: You command me to be strong and courageous. I will not be afraid or discouraged. I know that you are my God and are always with me.

OVERCOMING WEARINESS

Your Word says: "Come to me, all you who are weary and burdened, and I will give you rest" (Matt. 11:28 NIV).

I agree: I come to you when I am weary and burdened, and you give me rest.

Your Word says: "I will give those who are weary all they need. I will refresh everyone who is filled with sorrow" (Jer. 31:25 GW).

I agree: When I am weary, you give me all I need. You refresh me when I am filled with sorrow.

STABILITY

Your Word says: "He alone is my rock and my salvation, my fortress where I will never be shaken" (Ps. 62:2 NLT).

I agree: I will never be shaken because you alone, Lord, are my fortress, my rock, and my salvation.

Your Word says: "When the storm has swept by, the wicked are gone, but the righteous stand firm forever" (Prov. 10:25 NIV).

I agree: When the storms of life come, the wicked are swept away. Because you count me as righteous, Lord, I remain standing.

Your Word says: "I have set the LORD always before me; because he is at my right hand, I shall not be shaken" (Ps. 16:8 ESV).

I agree: I will focus on you, Lord. Because you are always beside me, I will not be shaken.

Dear Lord,

Thank you for these promises regarding strength, courage, stability, and overcoming weariness. I say yes and agree with them and believe they are for me. Give me even more faith to believe as I cling to your Word. I pray this in the power of the name of Jesus. Yes and amen.

25

Success

For nothing will be impossible with God.

Luke 1:37 ESV

Author Nick Harrison said, "Believing God's promises isn't an escape from reality or the troubles that plague us. But God's promises are stepping-stones for us to move on in life."[1]

My friend Carole Whang Schutter has found this to be true. One day she was driving though a Colorado mountain valley when, in her mind's eye, she saw a pioneer girl walking next to a covered wagon. Then the Lord began to talk to her about the girl, telling Carole that she was in a wagon train going to the California gold rush when she and the members of the train were attacked by white men dressed like Indians. Carole was amazed. She was even more amazed when God told her, "I want you to write her story."

"You mean a novel?" she asked.

"The screenplay," God replied.

Carole argued, "I don't know how to write a screenplay."

"Is that a problem? I do."

That's when Carole thought of her favorite Scripture verse: "For nothing will be impossible with God" (Luke 1:37 ESV).

When Carole began to research, she discovered that a young girl and her entire wagon train had indeed been murdered on September 11, 1857, by white men dressed like Indians in a Utah bloodbath called the Mountain Meadow Massacre.

Carole faithfully began to write their story, not sure if she was doing it "right."

Finally, she showed her story to her neighbor, Christopher Cain, the director of the film *Young Guns*. He was at first amused by Carole's screenwriting attempt, but then he became interested in the story.

The next thing Carole knew her screenplay was turned into the full-length feature movie *September Dawn*, directed by Christopher Cain and starring Jon Voight and Dean Cain.[2]

When you consider that only 1 percent of all screenwriters get their movies made, what happened to Carole is more than just a coincidence. It sounds to me as if Carole made a movie with God's help.

Author and pastor Erwin Lutzer noticed a couple of promises in Scripture that talk about success. He said:

> In each case the formula is the same. To Joshua, God said that if he would meditate in the book of the law day and night and be careful to do all that is written in it, "Then you will make your way prosperous, and then you will have good success" (Josh. 1:8). The same promise is given in Psalm 1 to all those who meditate in the law of God day and night: "He is like a tree planted by streams of water that yields its fruit in season, and its leaf does not wither. In all he does he prospers" (v. 3).[3]

Lutzer decided to experiment with this concept of finding success through meditating on God's Word. He picked a few Scripture passages to ponder each day, not worrying about trying to get God to answer his prayers or anything else. Lutzer wanted to meditate on God's Word daily as a way to honor him. The result? Lutzer noticed that things began to become easier for him, things such as preparing his sermons, writing, and staying on schedule.

Meditating on God's Word is a wonderful plan for success.

Name above All Names

One of God's names is *Elohim Ozer Li*, which means "God is my helper." David used this name of God when he wrote Psalm 54, saying in verse 4, "But God is my helper. The Lord keeps me alive!" (NLT).

David wrote this after the Ziphites told Saul where David was hiding. King Saul responded by sending three thousand men to kill David. But once again, God answered David's prayer for help. God put Saul and his men into such a deep sleep that evening that David was able to walk into their camp and steal Saul's spear and water jar. The next morning David chided Saul and his men for letting him get so close to the king. When Saul realized that David had not killed him when he'd had the chance, Saul once again repented for his murderous pursuit, at least for the moment.

You could say that David was an expert when it came to calling on God for help. He knew that God would come through for him and give him success, and this time was no different.

How about you? Have you called on God for help? What could you accomplish with God's help?

As we tour the promise garden of success, we will discover promises not only about success but also about:

- goals
- hard work
- perseverance/persistence

THE PROMISE GARDEN OF SUCCESS

Your Word says: "For I can do everything through Christ, who gives me strength" (Phil. 4:13 NLT).

I agree: There is nothing I can't do when Christ is in it.

Your Word says: "For nothing will be impossible with God" (Luke 1:37 ESV).

I agree: God, how wonderful that nothing is impossible with you.

Your Word says: "But Jesus looked at them and said, 'With man this is impossible, but with God all things are possible'" (Matt. 19:26 ESV).

I agree: What I hope to accomplish may not be possible through my own effort, but with you, Lord, all things are possible.

Your Word says: "For I know the plans I have for you, declares the Lord, plans for welfare and not for evil, to give you a future and a hope" (Jer. 29:11 ESV).

I agree: You have plans for me, God, not plans for evil but plans for provision, a future, and hope.

───

Your Word says: "This Book of the Law shall not depart from your mouth, but you shall meditate on it day and night, so that you may be careful to do according to all that is written in it. For then you will make your way prosperous, and then you will have good success" (Josh. 1:8 ESV).

I agree: I will quote your Word and your promises and meditate on them constantly. I will be careful to do all that your Word says. Then you, Lord, will make my way prosperous, and I will have good success.

───

Your Word says: "The blessing of the LORD makes a person rich, and he adds no sorrow with it" (Prov. 10:22 NLT).

I agree: Lord, you can make a person rich without adding sorrow to their abundance.

───

Your Word says: "Delight yourself in the LORD, and he will give you the desires of your heart" (Ps. 37:4 ESV).

I agree: I am delighted by you, Lord, and you give me the desires of my heart.

—

Your Word says: "Blessed is the person who does not follow the advice of wicked people, take the path of sinners, or join the company of mockers. Rather, he delights in the teachings of the LORD and reflects on his teachings day and night. He is like a tree planted beside streams—a tree that produces fruit in season and whose leaves do not wither. He succeeds in everything he does" (Ps. 1:1–3 GW).

I agree: I am blessed because I do not listen to the advice of wicked people who walk the path of sin, nor do I join those who mock others. Instead, I delight in God's Word and think about it day and night. I am like a tree planted by streams of water that produces fruit in its season. My leaves do not wither, and I succeed in everything I do.

GOALS

Your Word says: "Good planning and hard work lead to prosperity, but hasty shortcuts lead to poverty" (Prov. 21:5 NLT).

I agree: Planning and hard work lead to abundance, but questionable shortcuts lead to lack.

—

Your Word says: "And the Lord answered me: 'Write the vision; make it plain on tablets, so he may run who reads it. For still the vision awaits its appointed time; it hastens to the end—it will not lie. If it seems slow, wait for it; it will surely come; it will not delay'" (Hab. 2:2–3 ESV).

I agree: I will write down your goals for me, so I can run with them. The vision you give me will mature when its appointed time comes. Then there will be no delay in seeing your goals fulfilled.

—

Your Word says: "The heart of man plans his way, but the Lord establishes his steps" (Prov. 16:9 ESV).

I agree: I have my plans, but the Lord shows me how to take the right steps to reach my goals.

—

Your Word says: "Now to him who is able to do immeasurably more than all we ask or imagine, according to his power that is at work within us" (Eph. 3:20 NIV).

I agree: You, Lord, are able to do even more than I can ask or even imagine because of your great power working inside me. Thank you.

HARD WORK

Your Word says: "In the same way, faith by itself, if it is not accompanied by action, is dead" (James 2:17 NIV).

I agree: I will combine my faith with action because my faith is alive!

Your Word says: "But as for you, be strong and courageous, for your work will be rewarded" (2 Chron. 15:7 NLT).

I agree: I will be strong and courageous and will see my work rewarded.

Your Word says: "Whatever you do, work heartily, as for the Lord and not for men, knowing that from the Lord you will receive the inheritance as your reward. You are serving the Lord Christ" (Col. 3:23–24 ESV).

I agree: I am working for you, Lord. I will receive your reward.

Your Word says: "All hard work brings a profit, but mere talk leads only to poverty" (Prov. 14:23 NIV).

I agree: If I were all talk, I could find myself in lack, but I will work hard and make a profit.

Your Word says: "Whoever works his land will have plenty of bread, but he who follows worthless pursuits lacks sense" (Prov. 12:11 ESV).

I agree: I will not follow worthless pursuits. Instead, I will work hard and have plenty of provisions.

PERSEVERANCE/PERSISTENCE

Your Word says: "You need to persevere so that when you have done the will of God, you will receive what he has promised" (Heb. 10:36 NIV).

I agree: I will persevere so that when I have done what you have asked me, Lord, you will give me what you have promised.

Your Word says: "To those who by persistence in doing good seek glory, honor and immortality, he will give eternal life" (Rom. 2:7 NIV).

I agree: Because I persist in doing good and seek glory, honor, and immortality, you will give me eternal life.

Your Word says: "As you know, we count as blessed those who have persevered. You have heard of Job's perseverance and have seen what the Lord finally brought about. The Lord is full of compassion and mercy" (James 5:11 NIV).

I agree: Lord, you bless those who persevere, including Job. I believe you will show me compassion and mercy too.

Your Word says: "And let us not grow weary of doing good, for in due season we will reap, if we do not give up" (Gal. 6:9 ESV).

I agree: Lord, help me not to grow weary in doing good because I will succeed if I do not give up.

Your Word says: "And I am certain that God, who began the good work within you, will continue his work until it is finally finished on the day when Christ Jesus returns" (Phil. 1:6 NLT).

I agree: Lord, you have begun a good work in me, and I am grateful that you will continue this work until the day you return.

Dear Lord,

Thank you for these promises regarding success, goals, hard work, and perseverance/persistence. I say yes and agree with them and believe they are for me. Give me even more faith to believe as I cling to your Word. I pray this in the power of the name of Jesus. Yes and amen.

26

Troubles

Then call on me when you are in trouble,
and I will rescue you,
and you will give me glory.

Psalm 50:15 NLT

Corrie ten Boom once said, "Let God's promises shine on your problems."[1]

My friend Kathy wanted to believe that God's promises could shine on her trouble, but she was at the end of her rope. Her anger toward her two-year-old daughter, Darcy, was getting worse. "Oh, God," she prayed again and again, "deliver me from this anger right now! I'm afraid I'm going to kill Darcy in one of my rages."

She admitted, "I already constantly screamed at her, but my reactions were becoming more destructive, even to the point of choking her. But each prayer seemed like it bounced off the ceiling because nothing ever changed."

Whenever Kathy tried to figure out what caused her anger, she'd conclude, "It's Larry's fault!" Her husband, Larry, worked as a policeman and a real estate agent, had a flying hobby, and was never home. She said, "I hated him. If he would just stay home and help me, I wouldn't be acting like this."

It was easy for Kathy to blame him because she went to church, and he didn't. She led a women's neighborhood Bible study, and he only hung out with other officers.

While preparing to teach the neighborhood women one day, she studied Ephesians 3:20–21: "Now to him who is able to do far more abundantly than all that we ask or think, according to the power at work within us, to him be glory in the church and in Christ Jesus throughout all generations, forever and ever" (ESV).

Kathy said, "I stopped reading and felt frustrated. I prayed, 'Lord, this is saying, even promising, that you can do more than we ask. But it seems like you aren't even doing what I'm asking—taking away my anger. If you really are promising that you can take care of the worst kind of thing, like my anger, then bring glory to yourself through helping me.'"

She prayed sincerely, but she couldn't help but recognize that a part of her heart couldn't believe this promise fully.

Kathy said, "During one particularly angry day when I'd hurt Darcy again by kicking her, the verses seemed to mock me. I remembered that Larry had left his off-duty service revolver in the top dresser drawer. It seemed to call to me, and I thought, *I must take my life. Otherwise I'm going to kill Darcy.* But then the Spirit whispered, *But what will people think of Jesus if they hear that Kathy Miller has taken her life?* Only the thought of smudging Jesus's reputation made me not use that gun that day, even though I had no hope of deliverance."

But God was faithful. A few months later, God began the healing and deliverance process. God didn't answer Kathy's prayer for an instantaneous deliverance, but little by little over the following year, he revealed to her in many ways the reasons for her out-of-control anger and how to lay hold of his help. Kathy said, "Not only did I become a patient mom, but God also healed my marriage. Today Darcy is a forty-two-year-old mother and wife who calls me her best friend. Larry and I have been married almost fifty years, and he's my best friend."

Looking back, Kathy knows now that God's promise to do far more than we ask or imagine is true, even when he doesn't fulfill it exactly the way we think he should. She said, "If he can bring glory through my story and the ministry he's given me, then anyone in any situation can know that he will show himself faithful to fulfill the promise of Ephesians 3:20–21."[2]

Kathy is truly a woman who has been transformed by God, and it was this transformation that helped her conquer her anger and the trouble it caused.

Have you noticed that you never have to look far to find trouble? Author and pastor James MacDonald said, "Many people get hit by a wave of difficulty, followed by a tsunami that washes over them like a flood. Fine—have a day of that, but then rise to the surface, take hold of the promises of God, and ride the surf to shore. God will honor your faith. He's not going to let you drown."[3]

Name above All Names

Another name of God was given to him by a desperate young woman who had fled into the desert to escape her cruel mistress. It wasn't her fault that Sarai hadn't been able to conceive, nor was it her idea to be thrust into the arms of Sarai's husband, Abram.

But now, on the run, Hagar was dying of thirst in the desert.

The Lord himself heard her cries and came to her, saying, "You are now pregnant and will give birth to a son. You are to name him Ishmael (which means 'God hears'), for the LORD has heard your cry of distress" (Gen 16:11 NLT).

In response, Hagar called God *El Roi*, "the God who sees me." She told him, "I have now seen the One who sees me" (Gen. 16:13 NIV).

Be assured that God sees you in your troubles as well. He hears your cries, and he promises you hope and a future.

James MacDonald explained, "We must review his promises all the time. We must remind ourselves that our faith is in God who has never failed to do what He says. He knows what He has promised, He can't lie and He can't forget. He will deliver on time, all the time. Who else makes promises like that? The promises are great, the outcomes are certain; all that remains is to wait on God's timing."[4]

Let's review the promises God has given us regarding help and rescue in times of trouble.

THE PROMISE GARDEN FOR TROUBLES

Your Word says: "Dear brothers and sisters, when troubles of any kind come your way, consider it an opportunity for great joy. For you know that when your faith is tested, your endurance has a chance to grow. So let it grow, for when your endurance is fully developed, you will be perfect and complete, needing nothing" (James 1:2–4 NLT).

I agree: When troubles come my way, I consider it an opportunity for great joy, for when my faith is tested, my endurance grows.

When my endurance is fully developed, I will be perfect and complete and will not need anything.

—

Your Word says: "Praise be to the God and Father of our Lord Jesus Christ, the Father of compassion and the God of all comfort, who comforts us in all our troubles, so that we can comfort those in any trouble with the comfort we ourselves receive from God" (2 Cor. 1:3–4 NIV).

I agree: Praise be to you, God! You are the Father of our Lord Jesus Christ, the Father of all compassion and the God of all comfort. Because you comfort me in every trouble, I can comfort others with the same comfort I have received from you.

—

Your Word says: "We can rejoice, too, when we run into problems and trials, for we know that they help us develop endurance. And endurance develops strength of character, and character strengthens our confident hope of salvation" (Rom. 5:3–4 NLT).

I agree: Problems and trials are a blessing! They help me develop endurance, and endurance helps me develop strength of character, which in turn strengthens my confident hope of salvation.

—

Your Word says: "For our present troubles are small and won't last very long. Yet they produce for us a glory that vastly outweighs them and will last forever!" (2 Cor. 4:17 NLT).

I agree: My troubles are small and will not last long, but what glory they produce, glory that lasts forever.

—

Your Word says: "Blessed is the one who perseveres under trial because, having stood the test, that person will receive the crown of life that the Lord has promised to those who love him" (James 1:12 NIV).

I agree: I am blessed when I persevere under trial and remain faithful. I will receive the crown of life you have promised me because I love you.

—

Your Word says: "I've told you this so that my peace will be with you. In the world you'll have trouble. But cheer up! I have overcome the world" (John 16:33 GW).

I agree: Lord, thank you for your reassurance that your peace is with me. There is trouble in this world, but I am joyful! You have overcome the world.

—

Your Word says: "When the righteous cry for help, the Lord hears and delivers them out of all their troubles" (Ps. 34:17 ESV).

I agree: Thankfully, you count me as righteous, so when I cry for help, you hear me and deliver me out of my troubles.

—

Your Word says: "Because he holds fast to me in love, I will deliver him; I will protect him, because he knows my name. When he calls to me, I will answer him; I will be with him in trouble; I will rescue him and honor him" (Ps. 91:14–15 ESV).

I agree: I hold fast to you in love, and you will deliver me and protect me because I know your name. You always answer me when I call to you. You are always with me in trouble. How glad I am that you always rescue me and honor me.

~

Your Word says: "Then call on me when you are in trouble, and I will rescue you, and you will give me glory" (Ps. 50:15 NLT).

I agree: I am calling on you now. Help me! I know you will rescue me, and I will give you the glory.

~

Your Word says: "Let us then with confidence draw near to the throne of grace, that we may receive mercy and find grace to help in time of need" (Heb. 4:16 ESV).

I agree: Lord, I know I can draw near your throne of grace with confidence so that I can receive mercy and find help in my time of need.

~

Your Word says: "Now all glory to God, who is able, through his mighty power at work within us, to accomplish infinitely more than we might ask or think. Glory to him in the church and in

Christ Jesus through all generations forever and ever! Amen" (Eph. 3:20–21 NLT).

I agree: I praise you! You and your mighty power are more than able to work within me to accomplish so much more than I could think, ask, or imagine. May what you do for me bring glory to you, Jesus Christ, and to your church throughout all generations.

Your Word says: "The Lord will rescue me from every evil attack and will bring me safely to his heavenly kingdom. To him be glory forever and ever. Amen" (2 Tim. 4:18 NIV).

I agree: What would I do without your protection? You rescue me from every evil attack and bring me safely to your heavenly kingdom. To you be the glory forever and ever. Amen.

Your Word says: "God is our refuge and strength, a very present help in trouble" (Ps. 46:1 ESV).

I agree: You are my refuge and my strength. You are always present to help me when I'm in trouble.

Your Word says: "He has delivered us from such a deadly peril, and he will deliver us again. On him we have set our hope that he will continue to deliver us" (2 Cor. 1:10 NIV).

I agree: Lord, I know you will continue to deliver me. I know this because you have delivered me time and again. I base my hope on you alone.

⎯

Your Word says: "He sent from on high, he took me; he drew me out of many waters. He rescued me from my strong enemy and from those who hated me, for they were too mighty for me. They confronted me in the day of my calamity, but the LORD was my support. He brought me out into a broad place; he rescued me, because he delighted in me" (Ps. 18:16–19 ESV).

I agree: How glad I am that you delight in me. When I was drowning, you came down and rescued me from the strong enemy who hated me. Even though my enemy was too strong for me and attacked me when I was already in trouble, you, Lord, rescued me.

⎯

Dear Lord,

Thank you for these promises regarding the troubles in our lives. I say yes and agree with them and believe they are for me. Give me even more faith to believe as I cling to your Word. I pray this in the power of the name of Jesus. Yes and amen.

27

Worship

You have changed my sadness into a joyful dance; you
have taken away my sorrow and surrounded me with
joy. So I will not be silent; I will sing praise to you.
LORD, you are my God; I will give you thanks forever.

Psalm 30:11–12 GNT

Bible teacher Warren W. Wiersbe wrote these powerful words to
explain worship. He said:

How do you know what you are worshiping? The thing you work
for, sacrifice for and live for is your god. For some people, it's money.
For other people, it's possessions. With still others, it's ambition
or people. The psalmist shows us how foolish this is. Idols have
mouths, yet they can't make promises. But our God speaks to us,
and He gives us promises in His Word. Idols have eyes, but they
cannot see. They offer no protection. But "the eyes of the Lord are
on the righteous" (Ps. 34:15). God's eyes are watching us every moment of the day. He never goes to sleep. He cares for his children.

Idols have ears, but they cannot hear your prayers. If you talk to an idol, you are talking to yourself. But God's ears are open to our cries. He says, "Call to me and I will answer you" (Jer. 33:3).

The saddest thing about idolatry is that we become like the god we worship. . . . But if we worship the true and living God, we become like Him. We are transformed into the image of Jesus Christ.[1]

That is one powerful truth. Worship will align us with the true and living God like nothing else. Plus, worship is often the catalyst for answered prayer. Beyond that, worship makes our answered prayers more meaningful. Imagine how unsatisfying it would be to the Lord to grant an ungrateful heart its every request. Compare that with the pleasure God must feel when he grants the prayer requests of a person who delights in him and praises him for everything.

David was a young man who knew how to worship God, and he was a man whom God heard and answered when he prayed. Coincidence? Maybe not.

My friend Debbie Wilson understands the power of thanking God. She said, "Every time I slid behind the wheel of my car I gave thanks. The Lord had provided this used car at an affordable price at the perfect time. It was a direct answer to prayer. That's why I couldn't understand why he took it from me."

When a mission trip emptied her and her husband's pocketbooks, Larry's parents offered them the old, rusty Buick LeSabre that had belonged to Larry's late grandfather. Debbie said, "Larry accepted Granddad's car and sold mine to solve our financial shortfall. But besides being ugly, the car was unreliable."

Debbie thought her attitude about the car would improve after a church friend surprised them by providing a paint job and a new vinyl roof, but all she saw was the same dated monstrosity, though it was now green instead of yellow. It was simply not her car.

After dropping some students off one night, the Lord addressed Debbie's negative attitude by asking, *Have you thanked me for this car?*

Debbie told him, "How can I thank you when I'm not thankful?"

She said, "Instead of letting me off the hook, God filled my thoughts with Scripture. 'We know that God causes all things to work together for good to those who love God, to those who are called according to His purpose'" (Rom. 8:28 NASB).

Debbie's protests faded. By faith, she thanked God for her unwanted gift.

Months later, Debbie realized that her negative attitude toward the car had disappeared that night. And what do you know? The car no longer broke down!

When Debbie and Larry moved to northern Indiana, the green giant's spacious interior and smooth ride provided delightful transportation. It started every morning in below freezing temperatures, and its heater never failed. While fellow seminarians worried about salted roads tarnishing their cars, Debbie and her husband had no concerns.

Debbie said, "The gift I'd previously rejected taught me the value of trusting God's promises. It isn't hypocritical to thank God before we feel thankful. He always knows what's best for us."[2]

Debbie's worship and grateful heart added the finishing touches to the delight of God's provision of a car. I wonder if an attitude of gratitude would also bring life and joy to the provisions and miracles God has already put in our lives.

Max Lucado said, "Worship is the act of magnifying God. Enlarging our vision of him. Stepping into the cockpit to see where he sits and observe how he works. Of course, his size doesn't change, but our perception of him does. As we draw nearer, he seems larger. Isn't that what we need? A big view of God? Don't we have big problems, big worries, big questions? Of course we do. Hence we need a big view of God. Worship offers that."[3]

Name above All Names

David, in Psalm 109:1, called God *Elohei Tehillati*, meaning "the God of my praise," when he said, "My God, whom I praise, do not remain silent" (NIV).

It's significant that David praised God in this particular psalm, because his praise of the Lord was wrapped around a very long complaint about liars and the trouble they'd caused him.

Maybe you understand how it feels when people are unkind, unfair, and even dishonest, which is exactly what David was dealing with. But even though he was angry, David not only praised God but also called God the God of his praise!

In his love for David, God answered his prayers and defeated his foes.

What would happen in our lives if God became the God of our praise? I think our lives would be turned upside down.

Let's tour the promise garden of worship to see what promises the God of our praise has for us.

THE PROMISE GARDEN OF WORSHIP

Your Word says: "Praise the Lord; praise God our savior! For each day he carries us in his arms" (Ps. 68:19 NLT).

I agree: I praise you, Lord! I praise you, God my Savior! Thank you for daily carrying me in your arms. Thank you that you will never let me go.

Your Word says: "Give thanks to the LORD, for he is good; his love endures forever" (1 Chron. 16:34 NIV).

I agree: I give thanks to you, my wonderful Lord. You are good, and your love endures forever.

Your Word says: "Let them thank the LORD for his steadfast love, for his wondrous works to the children of man! For he satisfies the longing soul, and the hungry soul he fills with good things" (Ps. 107:8–9 ESV).

I agree: Lord, I thank you for your steadfast love, for your wondrous works in my life. You satisfy the longing of my soul. You fill my hungry soul with good things. I am satisfied in you.

Your Word says: "I call upon the LORD, who is worthy to be praised, and I am saved from my enemies" (2 Sam. 22:4 ESV).

I agree: You are worthy to be praised. When I call on you, Lord, you save me from my enemies.

Your Word says: "Worship the LORD your God, and his blessing will be on your food and water. I will take away sickness from among you" (Exod. 23:25 NIV).

I agree: I worship you, Lord, and you will bless my food and water and take sickness away from me.

Your Word says: "Praise the LORD, my soul! All my being, praise his holy name! Praise the LORD, my soul, and do not forget how kind he is. He forgives all my sins and heals all my diseases. He keeps me from the grave and blesses me with love and mercy. He fills my life with good things, so that I stay young and strong like an eagle" (Ps. 103:1–5 GNT).

I agree: I praise the Lord with all my soul! I praise your holy name! I do not forget how kind you are. You forgive all my sins and heal all my diseases. You keep me from the grave and bless me with love and mercy. You fill my life with good things so that I stay young and strong like an eagle.

Your Word says: "You have changed my sadness into a joyful dance; you have taken away my sorrow and surrounded me with joy. So I will not be silent; I will sing praise to you. LORD, you are my God; I will give you thanks forever" (Ps. 30:11–12 GNT).

I agree: You have changed my sadness into joy. You have taken away my sorrow and surrounded me with joy. How can I be quiet? I will sing praise to you, Lord, for you are my God. I will give thanks to you forever.

Your Word says: "All praise to God, the Father of our Lord Jesus Christ, who has blessed us with every spiritual blessing in the heavenly realms because we are united with Christ" (Eph. 1:3 NLT).

I agree: All praise to you, God, the Father of my Lord Jesus Christ. You have blessed me with every spiritual blessing in the heavenly realms because I am united with Christ.

———

Dear Lord,

Thank you for these promises regarding worship. I say yes and agree with them and believe they are for me. Give me even more faith to believe as I cling to your Word. I pray this in the power of the name of Jesus. Yes and amen.

Acknowledgments

Thank you, dear Revell, for the privilege of writing this joyful book, which also blessed my healing heart. Thanks to my family and to my dear husband, who has been a huge help and support. I'm also sending a shout out to my wonderful praying friends of the Advanced Writers and Speakers Association (AWSA). You rock! I so appreciate you all! And thanks to all my peeps, including Team Laura as well as Aisha.

Also, a special thanks to my editor, Vicki Crumpton, my agent, Janet Kobobel Grant, and all my wonderful friends at Baker Publishing Group, including Kristin Kornoelje. It has been such a blessing to partner with you in publishing this message of hope and promise.

I must also thank my dear readers. Please pray that this book will be a blessing to many who need the encouragement and hope it offers. Please consider sharing it with family, friends, and your community of believers.

I especially thank those who contributed stories. They include the following:

Janet Perez Eckles is an international speaker and an author of four books, including *Simply Salsa: Dancing without Fear at*

God's Fiesta. With engaging stories, this book invites you to find joy even in the midst of painful adversity. Read the first chapter here:

www.giftfromjanet.com

Carol Graham is the author of *Battered Hope*, a talk show host for *Never Ever Give Up Hope*, a keynote speaker, a business owner, and a certified health coach. She shares hope, encouragement, and laughter.

http://neverevergiveuphopenet.blogspot.com

Donna Hall is a grandmother who so appreciates that she can place her prayers in God's hands and trust in his timing. She says her grandchildren are a beautiful illustration of God's promises fulfilled.

Edie Melson—author, blogger, and speaker—has a passion to help those who are struggling find the God-given strength they need to triumph through difficult circumstances. Connect with her at:

www.EdieMelson.com

Kathy Collard Miller is an author of over fifty books, an international speaker, and a lay counselor. Her latest book is *Pure Hearted: The Blessings of Living Out God's Glory*.

www.KathyCollardMiller.com

Julie Morris is an internationally recognized author of twelve books and a popular motivational speaker. Her latest book, *Guided* *by Him . . . to a Thinner, Not So Stressed-Out You*, is a light and easy twelve-week Christian weight-loss program.

www.guidedbyhim.com

Karen Porter is an international speaker and businesswoman. She is the author of seven books, including *Speak like Jesus*. She and her husband, George, own Bold Vision Books, a Christian publishing company.

www.karenporter.com

Rhonda Rhea is a TV personality for CTN and a humor columnist. She has authored or coauthored twelve books, including *Fix-Her-Upper* and a novel, *Turtles in the Road*. Rhonda lives near St. Louis with her pastor hubby and has five grown children.

www.rhondarhea.com

Carole Whang Schutter is a screenwriter, a producer, and an author whose passion for history has led her into different genres. Born in Hawaii, she has lived half her life in Colorado.

www.cwschutter.com

Cynthia L. Simmons writes for *Leading Hearts* magazine. The author of *Pursuing Gold*, she hosts *Heart of the Matter Radio*, offering women the elegance of God's wisdom.

www.clsimmons.com.

Marilyn Turk is an award-winning author and speaker. She writes inspirational historical novels and devotions to encourage and motivate others to fulfill their God-given dreams. Read her blog at:

www.pathwayheart.com.

Marie Holcomb Underwood has four children and eight grandchildren. She and her husband reside in northeast Georgia and own Holcomb's Office Supply and Christian Products.

www.holcombsoffice.com

Karen Whiting is an international speaker, a former television host, and an author of twenty-five books. Her latest book, *The Gift of Bread*, provides heartwarming stories, recipes, and insights into bread in the Bible.

www.karenwhiting.com

Debbie W. Wilson speaks and writes to help others discover relevant faith. She is the author of *Little Women, Big God* and *Give Yourself a Break*. Share her journey to refreshing faith at:

www.debbieWwilson.com.

Also, a special thanks to Annie L. Goble, Bobbie Lemley, Terri and Dave Robinson, Marie Underwood, and all my silent contributors.

All of you played a part, and I am grateful.

Notes

Introduction

1. Nick Harrison, *Power in the Promises: Praying God's Word to Change Your Life* (Grand Rapids: Zondervan, 2013), 42.

Chapter 1: God's Powerful Promises

1. Andrew Murray, quoted in Thomas R. Yeakley, *Praying Over God's Promises: The Lost Art of Taking Him at His Word* (Colorado Springs: NavPress, 2015), 1.

Chapter 2: Answers to Prayer

1. Catherine Marshall, *Moments that Matter* (Nashville: Thomas Nelson, 2001), April 25.
2. Account based on work written and submitted by Marie Underwood. Used with permission.

Chapter 3: Blessings

1. Rebecka Barlow Jordan, *40 Days in God's Blessing* (New York: Warner Faith Hatchett Book Group, 2005), introduction.
2. Based on an interview with Karen Porter. Used with permission.
3. Mary Ruth Swope, *The Power of Blessing Your Children* (New Kensington, PA: Whittaker House, 2009), 22.

Chapter 4: Breakthroughs

1. Max Lucado, *The Applause of Heaven* (Nashville: Thomas Nelson, 2011), 88.
2. Based on an interview with Carole Whang Schutter. Used with permission.
3. Max Lucado, *He Still Moves Stones* (Nashville: Thomas Nelson, 1999), 59.

Chapter 5: Children

1. Swope, *The Power of Blessing Your Children*, 18.

Chapter 6: Comfort

1. Quote from Thomas Watson, from Steve Miller, *One Minute Promises of Comfort* (Eugene, OR: Harvest House, 2007), 9.
2. Miller, *One Minute Promises of Comfort*, 11.
3. Account based on work written and submitted by Bobbie Lemley. Used with permission.

Chapter 7: Deliverance

1. Account based on work written and submitted by Carol Graham. Used with permission.
2. Beth Moore, *Get Out of That Pit: Straight Talk about God's Deliverance* (Nashville: Thomas Nelson, 2007), 7.

Chapter 8: Direction

1. Account based on work written and submitted by Donna Hall, Amy's mother. Used with permission.
2. Marshall, *Moments that Matter*, May 20.

Chapter 9: Faith

1. Sheila Walsh, *The Shelter of God's Promises Participant's Guide* (Nashville: Thomas Nelson, 2010), 22.
2. Account based on work written and submitted by Marilyn Turk. Used with permission.
3. R. C. Sproul, *The Promises of God: Discovering the One Who Keeps His Word* (Colorado Springs: David C. Cook, 2013), 8.

Chapter 10: Faithfulness of God

1. Sproul, *The Promises of God*, 8.
2. Carol Kent and Jennie Afman Dimkoff, *Miracle on Hope Hill* (New York: Howard Books, 2011), 143–45.
3. Sproul, *The Promises of God*, 8.

Chapter 11: Godliness

1. Account based on work written and submitted by Julie Morris. Used with permission.
2. Rhonda Harrington Kelley, *Divine Discipline: How to Devlop and Maintain Self-Control* (Gretna, LA: Pelican Publishing Group, 1995), 35.

Chapter 12: Healing

1. Andrew Murray, *Divine Healing* (Abbotsford, WI: Aneko Press, 2016), front matter.
2. Murray, *Divine Healing*, front matter.
3. Murray, *Divine Healing*, 3.
4. Account based on work written and submitted by Carol Graham. Used with permission.
5. Murray, *Divine Healing*, 104.

Chapter 13: Heaven

1. Don Piper quote, John Burke, *Imagine Heaven* (Grand Rapids: Baker Books, 2015), 13.

Chapter 14: Hope

1. Anne Graham Lotz quote, Jack Countryman and Terri Gibbs, *God's Promises Day by Day: 365 Days of Inspirational Thoughts* (Nashville: Thomas Nelson, 2003), 65.
2. Account based on work written and submitted by Janet Perez Eckles. Used with permission.
3. Corrie ten Boom, *Each New Day* (Grand Rapids: Revell, 2003), 61.

Chapter 15: Joy

1. Alicia Britt Chole quote, Countryman and Gibbs, *God's Promises Day by Day*, 32.
2. Charles Swindoll, *Laugh Again* (Nashville: Thomas Nelson, 1992), 29.

Chapter 16: Love

1. Billy Graham, *Peace with God* (Nashville: Thomas Nelson, 2011), 39.
2. Annie's story shared with permission.
3. James Bryan Smith, *Embracing the Love of God: Path and Promise of Christian Life* (Grand Rapids: Zondervan, 1995), 3.

Chapter 17: Peace

1. Max Lucado, *Traveling Light* (Nashville: Thomas Nelson, 2006), 75.
2. Ann Spangler, *The Peace God Promises* (Grand Rapids: Zondervan, 2014), 30.
3. Harrison, *Power in the Promises*, 19.

Chapter 18: Presence of God

1. Account based on work written and submitted by Cynthia L. Simmons. Used with permission.
2. Henry Blackaby and Richard Blackaby, *Discovering God's Daily Agenda* (Nashville: Thomas Nelson, 2007), 37.

Chapter 19: Protection

1. Walsh, *The Shelter of God's Promises Participant's Guide*, 14.
2. Based on an interview with Rhonda Rhea. Used with permission.

Chapter 20: Provision

1. Walsh, *The Shelter of God's Promises Participant's Guide*, 47.
2. Account based on work written and submitted by Karen Whiting. Used with permission.
3. Walsh, *The Shelter of God's Promises*, 33.

Chapter 21: Purpose

1. Linda Evans Shepherd, *Winning Your Daily Spiritual Battles* (Grand Rapids: Revell, 2016), 20.
2. Shepherd, *Winning Your Daily Spiritual Battles*, 20.

Chapter 22: Relationships

1. Janet Kobobel Grant, *Growing in Prayer* (Grand Rapids: Zondervan, 1998), 74.
2. Based on an interview with Dawn. Used with permission.
3. The Google online dictionary.
4. Max Lucado, *Pocket Prayers for Military Life: 40 Simple Prayers that Bring Faith and Courage* (Nashville: Thomas Nelson, 2016), 22.

Chapter 23: Salvation

1. Billy Graham, "Sinner's Prayer," Wikipedia, https://en.wikipedia.org/wiki /Sinner%27s_prayer.
2. Account based on work written and submitted by Edie Melson. Used with permission.

Chapter 24: Strength

1. Charles F. Stanley, *Waiting on God* (New York: Howard Books, 2015), 198.

Chapter 25: Success

1. Harrison, *Power in the Promises*, 20.
2. Based on an interview with Carole Whang Schutter. Used with permission.
3. Erwin W. Lutzer, *Failure: The Back Door to Success* (Chicago: Moody, 2016), 130.

Chapter 26: Troubles

1. Corrie ten Boom, *The One Year Praying the Promises of God* (Carol Stream, IL: Tyndale, 2012), February 6.

2. Account based on work written and submitted by Kathy Collard Miller. Used with permission.

3. James MacDonald, *Always True: God's 5 Promises When Life Is Hard* (Chicago: Moody, 2011), 23.

4. MacDonald, *Always True*, 21.

Chapter 27: Worship

1. Warren W. Wiersbe, *Prayer, Praise, and Promises* (Grand Rapids: Baker Books, 2011), 343.

2. Account based on work written and submitted by Debbie Wilson. Used with permission.

3. Max Lucado, *The Lucado Life Lessons Study Bible* (Nashville: Thomas Nelson, 2010), 799.

Linda Evans Shepherd is an award-winning author of over thirty books, including the bestselling *When You Don't Know What to Pray* and *Winning Your Daily Spiritual Battles* (which won a 2017 EIE Award and was a 2017 Selah finalist).

Linda is an internationally recognized speaker and has spoken in almost every state in the United States and in several countries around the world.

She is the president of Right to the Heart Ministries and the CEO of the Advanced Writers and Speakers Association (AWSA), which ministers to Christian women authors and speakers. See www.AWSA.com and AWSAProtege.com. She's both the publisher of *Leading Hearts Magazine*, www.LeadingHearts.com, and AriseDaily, www.AriseDaily.com, a daily e-devotional written by the members of AWSA.

Linda loves to hang out with friends and family and has been married to Paul for over thirty years. She is the mother of two wonderful kids, one in Austin and the other in heaven.

To learn more about Linda's ministries, go to www.GotToPray .com. Follow Linda on Twitter at @LindaShepherd or on Facebook at www.facebook.com/GotToPray/.

Transform Your Life through Prayer with Linda Evans Shepherd

Visit **GotToPray.com** to receive a FREE prayer toolbox, find printable prayers, submit a prayer request, and learn more about Linda's SPEAKING and BLOGGING.

 Linda Evans Shepherd   @LindaShepherd

g Linda Evans Shepherd   Linda Evans Shepherd

DISCOVER HOW TO TAME YOUR STRESS, STILL YOUR FEARS, AND CALM YOUR HEART.

"Packed with prayer and promises, this book will free you to experience the power of God's peace."

—LYSA TERKEURST,
New York Times bestselling author of *Uninvited*
and president of Proverbs 31 Ministries

MAYBE YOU OR SOMEONE YOU KNOW IS IN DESPERATE NEED OF A MIRACLE.

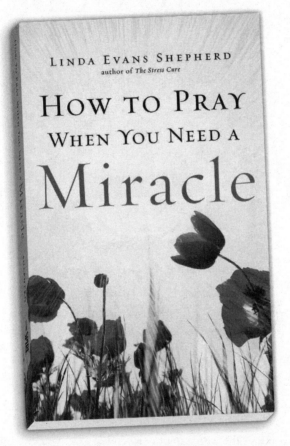

In this powerful book, Linda Evans Shepherd shows you how to reach out to God and simply ask—with confidence and expectation. God's answers may not always come packaged in the ways you expect, but they do come in ways that will transform your life. Through solid biblical teaching and dramatic real-life stories, Shepherd walks with you on a journey of renewed hope and the assurance that God still works miracles.

Do you ever not know what to say to God?

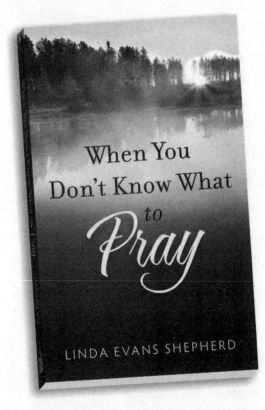

How do you find the words to pray when life gives you circumstances beyond your control? When your finances, family, health, work, and more have driven you to a place of confusion? When it seems like the easiest thing would be to simply give up? Linda Evans Shepherd knows what it's like to desperately seek God through prayer. As she takes you through her own journey and the true stories of others, you will be encouraged and equipped to pray for yourself in any circumstance.

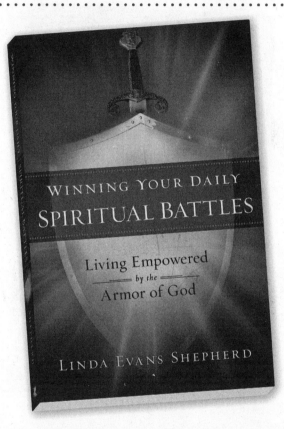

NO MATTER WHAT THE HURT, THERE IS ALWAYS, *ALWAYS* HOPE.

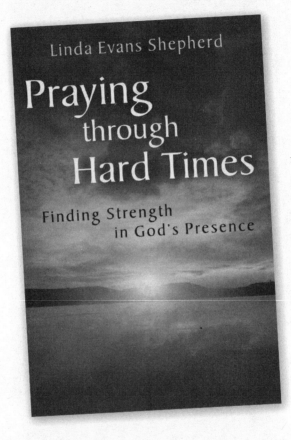

In *Praying through Hard Times*, Linda Evans Shepherd shows you how to see God in times of trouble. With compassion born from her own experiences with tragedy, Shepherd offers you practical strategies for surviving difficult times, giving your worries and sadness to God, praying through the pain, and finding peace, hope, and joy once more.

 **Revell**
a division of Baker Publishing Group
www.RevellBooks.com

Available wherever books and ebooks are sold.

When you feel a nudge to pray, what will you do?

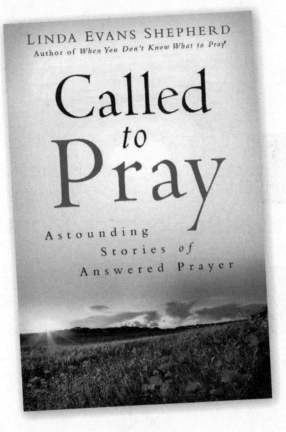

In *Called to Pray*, Linda Evans Shepherd shares dozens of inspiring true stories of people who have heeded God's call to pray and the astonishing results of those impromptu prayers. Through accounts of people being protected from harm and rescued from danger, of needs being met and hearts being encouraged, you'll see that God is involved in an active and dynamic relationship with us—and that we can be part of his plan to bless others.